A BIBLIOGRAPHY OF

SHIP PASSENGER LISTS, 1538–1825

A BIBLIOGRAPHY OF

SHIP PASSENGER LISTS

1538–1825

*Being a Guide to Published Lists of
Early Immigrants to North America*

Compiled by HAROLD LANCOUR

THIRD EDITION
Revised and Enlarged by RICHARD J. WOLFE

WITH A LIST OF
PASSENGER ARRIVAL RECORDS IN THE NATIONAL ARCHIVES
By FRANK E. BRIDGERS

New York
The New York Public Library

Library of Congress Catalogue Card Number: 63–18141

*   *   *

A revised edition of

Passenger Lists of Ships Coming to North America, 1607–1825

(1938)

Illustrations by HAL WILSON, Public Relations Staff

Second, corrected printing
Printed by offset
form p717 [viii-1-66 2m]

Preface to the Third Edition

OF INESTIMABLE VALUE to genealogists and historians would be a record of every emigrant who sailed from Europe to North America in the early years of our nation's history. But no such record exists. Actually, the ravages of fire and time have left to succeeding generations but little of the all too incomplete documents made by the shipping and port authorities in those early days. Those that do remain are now preserved in the archives and libraries of the United States and Europe.

In recent years efforts have been made to sort out, transcribe, and print from such old original records, diaries, log books, etc, lists of the early emigrants. This bibliography is an attempt to bring together a list of these printed sources and to put it into a convenient and usable form. Word has reached us from many places that the earlier editions of this little pamphlet, which first appeared in 1938, have indeed been found useful far beyond our most hopeful expectations.

The emphasis in this compilation has been utilitarian rather than academic. Its purpose is to provide genealogists, historians, and students of immigration with a useful guide to widely scattered and little-known material. Such emphasis has had two results: first, to make advisable a free interpretation of the phrase "passenger list" so as to include all such collections of emigrants' or immigrants' names, as, in the opinion of the compiler, would be of value; and, second, to call for a simple bibliographical entry with a briefly descriptive rather than evaluative annotation.

On the assumption that the researcher, in looking for a particular individual's name, will know at least one of three things: the place of arrival, the approximate date of arrival, or the name of the ship, the list is arranged, first by the state to which the ship came, and second, under each state, chronologically by the year of arrival. In addition there is a complete index to all ships' names mentioned in the several books and articles listed in the bibliography giving exact page references to the books and articles referred to.

A few users of the original edition of this work kept records of additional items which subsequently were published or came to light. Mr Richard J. Wolfe, of The New York Public Library staff, has kindly brought these and a great many other supplementary materials together and incorporated them into the bibliography and the index. Thus the list is as complete, up to the time of publication, as cooperative effort can make it. As before, additions and corrections to the list will be appreciated and may be sent to the compiler or to The New York Public Library.

HAROLD LANCOUR

Morgan Hill Farm
Weston, Vermont

Reviser's Preface

TO THOSE engaged in the study of American genealogy and immigration Harold Lancour's *Passenger Lists* will require no introduction. Since its publication by The New York Public Library 26 years ago as a modest booklet it has achieved a remarkable reputation as one of the most useful tools for aiding in the identification of persons coming to North America before 1825, and the demand for copies of it has not diminished over the years in spite of the fact that it has long since gone out of print. The usefulness of the Lancour *Bibliography* lies not only in bringing together references to so many scattered lists but in the utilitarian manner in which it has organized and presented them.

It has been my intention in undertaking the revision and enlargement of *Passenger Lists* to preserve as much as possible the identity and practical intent of the original. Only such changes and modifications have been adopted as would improve upon the aim and usefulness of the work or which seemed necessary in order to incorporate into it the many items which have appeared in print since 1938. The standard for including a list in the revised edition is *proof of overseas origin.* I have reserved the right of judgment in this matter, as did Dr Lancour before me, *usefulness* being the deciding factor in borderline cases. And again no claim is made for unerring judgment or for completeness, though I have made every effort to make the present edition as complete and comprehensive as possible.

Every entry appearing in the second edition of *Passenger Lists* (1938) has been described anew and has been completely reindexed for inclusion in the "Index of Ship Names" at the end of the volume. And to these have been added approximately 145 new references. A number of typographical errors and errors of oversight have been corrected, and every reference has been annotated in order to inform the user of the origin and scope of each entry within the volume. The section "Name Registers and Genealogical Dictionaries" found at the conclusion of the earlier list has been dropped out and two appendices, one giving lists of ship passengers and immigrants coming to America after 1825 and the other passenger arrival records in the National Archives, have been substituted in its place. By doing this we hope to furnish the user with a compendium of all known published passenger and immigrant records and at the same time provide him with a résumé of the holdings of our major source of such unpublished data. (For the type of material originally included in "Name Registers and Genealogical Dictionaries," where proof of overseas origin is not established, the reader is directed to various genealogical handbooks, such as *Genealogical Research* and *Search and Research*, which usually include such materials under their respective states.) [1] To add to the usefulness of the work, a number of cross references have been inserted in order to inform the user of regional material included in lists entered under different localities; an author index has also been furnished; and slight changes have been made in the manner of entering references in the analytical index of ship names. I have tried to take notice of all reprinted editions of works in the *Bibliography* so as to tell the researcher what may be purchased on the "in print" market. The majority of such reprints have been issued by the Genealogical Publishing Company, 521–23 St Paul Place, Baltimore, and, as I have been informed by Mr Jules Chodak, President of the firm, as many more will be scheduled for republication in the future as demand warrants. Finally, the work has been given a new title which, it is hoped, will better reflect the true nature of its contents and will help abate the confusion that the earlier title created.

As Dr Lancour implies in his preface to this edition, its undertaking has been a cooperative effort. I should like to express my gratitude for the kind assistance rendered by Dr Gerald D. McDonald of this Library and by the staff of the Genealogy and Local History Division which he heads, and particularly by Mr Gunther E. Pohl,

---

[1] *Genealogical Research: Methods and Sources* (Washington, D C, The American Society of Genealogists 1960); Noel C. Stevenson *Search and Research; The Researcher's Handbook* (Salt Lake City, Deseret Book Co 1959).

who read over the manuscript and made a number of valuable suggestions, and by Miss Rosalie Fellows Bailey, who went over the New York and New Jersey sections and offered a great many references for my consideration. I should also like to thank Mr Frank E. Bridgers for contributing his article "Passenger Arrival Records in the National Archives," which originally appeared in the *National Genealogical Society Quarterly* for September 1962, and Colonel Carleton E. Fisher, President of the Society, for permitting it to be republished. Finally I would like to acknowledge the interest of Mr Jules Chodak, and the assistance rendered by him in the course of this revision.

RICHARD J. WOLFE

The New York
Public Library

Contents

PREFACE TO THE THIRD EDITION   v

REVISER'S PREFACE   vii

THE BIBLIOGRAPHY

    ALL PORTS   3
    MAINE   13
    NEW HAMPSHIRE   15
    MASSACHUSETTS   17
    RHODE ISLAND   25
    CONNECTICUT   27
    NEW YORK   29
    NEW JERSEY   41
    PENNSYLVANIA   45
    DELAWARE   63
    MARYLAND   65
    VIRGINIA   69
    DISTRICT OF COLUMBIA   75
    NORTH CAROLINA   77
    SOUTH CAROLINA   79
    GEORGIA   81
    FLORIDA   83
    LOUISIANA   85

APPENDIX I: PUBLISHED LISTS OF SHIP PASSENGERS
    AND IMMIGRANTS AFTER 1825   87

APPENDIX II: PASSENGER ARRIVAL RECORDS IN THE
    NATIONAL ARCHIVES, BY FRANK E. BRIDGERS   93

INDEX OF AUTHORS AND CONTRIBUTORS   101

INDEX OF SHIP NAMES   105

A Bibliography of
Ship Passenger Lists, 1538-1825

ALL PORTS

1600–1700

John Camden Hotten, ed, *The Original Lists of Persons of Quality; Emigrants; Religious Exiles; Political Rebels; Serving Men Sold for a Term of Years; Apprentices; Children Stolen; Maidens Pressed; and Others Who Went from Great Britain to the American Plantations, 1600–1700. With Their Ages, the Localities Where They Formerly Lived in the Mother Country, the Names of the Ships in Which They Embarked, and Other Interesting Particulars. From Mss. Preserved in the State Paper Department of Her Majesty's Public Record Office, England* (London, Chatto and Windus 1874) 604 p **1**

Very comprehensive. Includes lists of ships to Bermuda and the Barbados as well as to North America. Contains an index to all family names.

Published also, New York, J. W. Bouton 1874. Second American ed published 1880 under title *Our Early Immigrant Ancestors. The Original Lists of Persons of Quality.* . . . Second ed of 1880 reissued in facsimile by the Genealogical Publishing Co, Baltimore, 1962.

For an excerpt of the names of Jews appearing in this list see Cyrus Adler, "Jews in American Plantations between 1600–1700," *Publications of the American Jewish Historical Society* I (1893) 105–108.

See note for no 35.

1600–1750

"Immigrants to America before 1750; an Alphabetical List of Immigrants to the Colonies, before 1750, Compiled from Official and Other Records," *The Magazine of American Genealogy* sec IV nos 1–27 (1929–1932) 220 p **2**

An ambitious attempt to list all known immigrants to America before 1750, gathered from a variety of sources including personal genealogies, state archives, colonial records, state and local histories, etc, and correlating the records of several colonies.

Published as Section IV of each of the first 27 issues of the magazine with its own title-page and with separate paging. Suspended publication with no 27, and consequently only carried emigrants to America whose surnames begin with the letter "A" or the letter "B" through "Battles."

"Immigrant Ancestors" (*In* Frederick A. Virkus, ed *The Abridged Compendium of American Genealogy,* Chicago, The Institute of American Genealogy 1925–1942, I 965–997, II 387–421, III 645–692, IV 727–777, V 741–793, VI 749–818, VII 825–895) **3**

A major source of information on several thousand immigrants to America before 1750, giving birth, ancestry, time and place of arrival, and marriage and death of each immigrant.

The section in each volume is complete in itself, running alphabetically A through Z. Names in these sections of "Immigrant Ancestors" appear in the alphabetical index at

All Ports, 1600–1750, continued

the back of each volume. The section in vol vii, which appears to be the most complete, has been reissued in facsimile by the Genealogical Publishing Co, Baltimore, in 1963.

Because a great percentage of entries are repeated in succeeding volumes and because an even greater number of immigrant ancestors are mentioned in the lineage records in the main section of each volume, ship names occurring here have not been included in the Index of Ship Names below.

A more complete list of immigrants to America before 1750 whose surname begins with the letter A or the letter B through "Battles" is contained in no 2.

1600–1800

George Sherwood, *American Colonists in English Records. A Guide to Direct References in Authentic Records, Passenger Lists not in "Hotten," &c., &c., &c.* Series 1–2 (London, G. Sherwood 1932–1933) 2 v	**4**

A highly miscellaneous collection of items found in English records. Arrangement is by date, with an index of names contained in both series following at end of vol ii.
Reissued in facsimile by the Genealogical Publishing Co, Baltimore, 1961.

1620–1650

Charles Edward Banks, *Topographical Dictionary of 2885 English Emigrants to New England, 1620–1650.* Edited, Indexed and Published by Elijah Ellsworth Brownell, B. E. E. (Philadelphia 1937) 295 p	**5**

Comprehensive listing of early emigrants from England arranged by county and parish of origin, with name of ship, place of settlement in this country and authority cited. Contains alphabetical indices of emigrants and wives and children of emigrants and indices of parishes in England whence they emigrated, towns in the colonies in which they settled, and the ships they arrived in.
Reissued in facsimile by the Genealogical Publishing Co, Baltimore, 1957.

1631–1635

Charles B. Moore, "Shipwrights, Fishermen, Passengers from England," *The New York Genealogical and Biographical Record* x (1879) 66–76	**7**

A general article on the first settlers of New England, Virginia, and New York, but contains the names of several dozen emigrants to New England, Virginia, New York, and the American or West Indian Islands extracted from ms volumes kept in London to preserve oaths of allegiance required of English soldiers and passengers going abroad.

1634–1635

Arthur Adams, "Adams Emigration Lists, 1572–1640; England," *National Genealogical Society Quarterly* ix (1920) 38–39	**8**

A list of emigrants from England whose surname was *Adams, Adam, Haddam*, etc, culled from contemporary ms emigrations lists from the 14th year of Queen Elizabeth (1572) to 1640. Includes a number of persons bound for New England and Virginia, 1634–1635.

1635–1640

Vincent B. Redstone, "American Traders, Planters and Settlers. Notes Drawn from Original Papers, 1628–1640," *Genealogical Magazine* III (1916) 139–144 **9**

A general account, based on old public documents, of expeditions from England to the New World, 1628–1640. Includes 3 short lists.

1646–1775

Anthony J. Camp, "Transportation from Hertfordshire, England to America, 1646–1775," *The New England Historical and Genealogical Register* CXV (1961) 55–57 **10**

Extracted from the 10 volumes of printed *Hertfordshire Quarter Sessions Records* (1905–1957).

A list of convicts deported from Hertfordshire during the period covered. Gives name, place of origin, occupation, and year of deportation and is coded to designate destination to be America, Virginia or Maryland, Barbados, or Jamaica.

No ship mentioned.

1654–1685

Bristol, England, *Bristol and America; a Record of the First Settlers in the Colonies of North America, 1654–1685, Including the Names with Places of Origin of More Than 10,000 Servants to Foreign Plantations Who Sailed from the Port of Bristol to Virginia, Maryland, and Other Parts of the Atlantic Coast, and Also to the West Indies from 1654 to 1685* (London, R. S. Glover [1929]) 182 p **11**

An important collection of the names enrolled in two volumes, "Servants to Foreign Plantations," found among the archives of Bristol, England. Records emigrants to New England, Maryland, Virginia, New York, Pennsylvania, and to Canada and the Caribbean Islands.

"Compiled and published from their records by special permission of the Corporation of the City of Bristol." Preface by N. Dermott Harding, Keeper of the Bristol Archives; Historical Introduction by Wm. Dodgson Bowman; transcriptions by R. Hargreaves-Mawdsley.

A printed index of names, consisting of a cover-title and 16 pages, was issued separately by the publisher in 1931 and is found in most copies sold after that date. Title to this commences *An Index to Bristol and America* . . . and repeats t-p information of the book, but has price added and imprint altered. A ms index of 158 leaves, "giving names of settlers and ships [with] references to the destination 'New England' . . . starred," was compiled by Margaret MacKinnon Lorenz, Boston, in 1929. Photostat reproductions of this can be found in various libraries (Boston Athenaeum, New York Historical Society, The New York Public Library, etc).

P 1–26 of Book I of "Servants to Foreign Plantations" also printed in R. Hargreaves-Mawdsley, "The Bristol Records; a Representative List of Names of Persons Who Emigrated to America between the Years 1654 and 1679," *Apollo: a Journal of the Arts* VI (1927) 29–31.

See also nos 55 and 199.

1680–1820

"Names of Some Ministers, Licentiates, Students, or Emigrants Who Went from Ulster and Served in the Ministry of Presbyterian Churches in North America during the Period 1680–1820, with the Presbytery of Oversight, or District of Origin Where These Have Been Ascertained, the Date or Approximate Date of Arrival, and the Provinces or States Where They Exercised Their Ministry" (*In* William Forbes Marshall *Ulster Sails West,* Belfast, The Quota Press [1943] p 60–67)   **11-1**

Arranged alphabetically. No ship mentioned.

1683–1684

Cregoe D. P. Nicholson, "Some Early Emigrants to America," *Genealogists' Magazine* xii (1955–1958) 11–14, 48–53, 89–92, 122–125, 157–162, 191–196, 228–233, 269–272, 303–309, 340–344, 379–382, 404–406, 440–442, 478–482, 516–520, 552–555; xiii (1959–1961) 10–13, 46–50, 78–80, 105–108, 145–148, 175–179, 209–212, 236   **12**

Lists approximately 1,000 persons who indentured themselves to serve in the plantations in 1683 and 1684, mainly in Maryland, Virginia, Barbados, and Jamaica, though a few were destined for New York, New Jersey, Pennsylvania, and Carolina. Gives the name of the apprentice, the town from which he came, his occupation and his age; the name, address, and occupation of the person to whom the apprentice was bound (usually the master of the ship); the place to which he was going, the number of years he was bound, the ship in which he was to sail, and the name of the ship's master.

1690–1811

Gerald Fothergill, *A List of Emigrant Ministers to America, 1690–1811* (London, Elliot Stock 1904) 65 p   **13**

An alphabetical list of ministers and schoolmasters of the Church of England who went to western colonies in return for a bounty of twenty pounds from the King.

From Money Books, King's Warrant Books, Treasury Papers, and Exchequer of Receipt Papers in the Public Record Office, London.

Gives name of minister, his destination, and the date of payment of bounty.

See *The New England Historical and Genealogical Register* lix (1905) 218–219 for additions.

1697–1707

Elizabeth French, *List of Emigrants to America from Liverpool, 1697–1707* (Boston, New England Historic Genealogical Society 1913) 55 p   **14**

From the Records of the Corporation of Liverpool.

A chronological arrangement of over 1,500 names of indentured servants destined for Virginia, Maryland, Pennsylvania, New England, and the West Indies. Gives name, age, period of indenture, and the person to whom indentured, frequently the master of the ship on which he sailed.

Contains an index of names.

Reprinted in facsimile from   *14A The New England Historical and Genealogical Register* LXIV (1910) 158–166, 252–263, 336–346; LXV (1911) 43–50, 165–174.
Reissued in facsimile by the Genealogical Publishing Co, Baltimore, 1962.

1697–1815

"Tabelle der Auswanderer des 17. und 18. Jahrhunderts. a. Die Auswanderer nach Amerika" (*In* Robert Mörsdorf *Die Auswanderung aus dem Birkenfelder Land,* Bonn, Ludwig Röhrscheid Verlag 1939, p 87–91)   *15*

A chronological register of emigrants to America from the principality of Birkenfeld during the 17th and 18th centuries. Contains a great many immigrants to Pennsylvania.

1709

William J. Hoffman, " 'Palatine' Emigrants to America from the Principality of Nassau-Dillenburg," *The National Genealogical Society Quarterly* XXIX (1941) 41–44   *16*

From records in the State Archives at Wiesbaden.
A general article discussing and reprinting petitions written during July and Aug 1709 by subjects of the Count of Nassau-Dillenburg praying to be permitted to leave for America.
Contains the names of 54 persons petitioning to go to Pennsylvania or the Carolinas. Gives name only.
Based on an article which appeared in the German local magazine *Nassovia* IV (1903) 194ff.
Printed in part in no 137.

1727–1895

"Auswanderung" (*In* Albrecht Ritz *Gestalten und Ereignisse aus Beihingen am Neckar.* Ludwigsburg, Buchdruckerei Otto Eichhorn 1939, p 238–258)   *16-1*

Contains the names of emigrants from Beihingen to America during the period covered.

1738

Friedrich Krebs, "Amerika-Auswanderer aus Baden-Durlach im Jahre 1738," *Senftenegger Monatsblatt für Genealogie und Heraldik* IV (1956–1959) 17–18   *17*

Compiled from documents in the Badischen Generallandesarchiv in Karlsruhe.
Contains names only of persons granted permission to emigrate to America.
No ship mentioned.

1738–1750

Paul W. Prindle, "Some Emigrants to America from the Ludwigsburg District, Wurttemberg, Germany, 1738–1750," *The New York Genealogical and Biographical Record* XCIII (1962) 65–66   *17-1*

All Ports, 1738–1750, continued

From archives of the City Council of Poppenweiler, Ludwigsburg District.
The names of 13 families who declared their intentions to emigrate to America,
Pennsylvania, or New York.

1740–1757

Jacob Harry Hollander, "The Naturalization of Jews in the American Colonies under the Act of 1740," *Publications of the American Jewish Historical Society* v (1897)103–117   **18**

Transcribed from records of the Commissioners for Trade and Plantations now
among the documents of the Colonial Office in the Public Record Office, London.
Contains the names of Jews naturalized in South Carolina, Pennsylvania, Maryland
and New York during the period covered.
Also printed in no 19.
See note for no 102.

1740–1772

Montague Spencer Giuseppi, ed, *Naturalizations of Foreign Protestants
in the American and West Indian Colonies Pursuant to Statute 13 George
II, c. 7* (Manchester, The Huguenot Society of London 1921) 196 p   **19**

Volume xxiv of *The Publications of The Huguenot Society of London.*
Contains all the returns of naturalization of foreign Protestants sent from the
Colonies to the Lords Commissioners for Trade and Plantations during the period
covered.
Transcribed from 2 Entry Books formerly belonging to the Board of Trade and
Plantations but now classified among documents of the Colonial Office in the Public
Record Office, London.
Amount of information given differs according to Colony, but entries usually include
name, religious affiliation, place of residence, and date of naturalization. Returns from
New York usually include occupation.
Contains returns from the West Indies, South Carolina, North Carolina, Virginia,
Maryland, New York, and Pennsylvania.
Has indices of persons, places, and subjects (denominations, occupations, etc.)
See note for no 102.

1752–1900

"Vor der Auswanderer aus dem Heidenheimer Gebiet" (*In* Albrecht Ritz
Nattheim und Oggenhausen im Kranz der Nachbargemeinden. Heiden-
heim/Brenz, Heidenheimer Verlagsanstalt 1951, p 231–245)   **19-1**

A record of emigrants to America from Nattheim, Oggenhausen, and Fleinheim during the period covered.

1773–1776

Gerald Fothergill, *Emigrants from England, 1773–1776* (Boston, New
England Historic Genealogical Society 1913) 206 p   **20**

A list of about 6,000 names, copied from Treasury Records in the Public Record
Office, London. Gives information concerning the age, occupation, point, of origin,

ship, destination, and reason for emigrating of each passenger in convenient tabulated form, arranged chronologically.

Includes ships to all parts of North America.

Reprinted from   *20A* Gerald Fothergill, "Emigrants from England," *The New England Historical and Genealogical Register* LXII (1908) 242–253, 320–332; LXIII (1909) 16–31, 134–146, 234–244, 342–355; LXIV (1910) 18–25, 106–115, 214–227, 314–326; LXV (1911) 20–35, 116–132, 232–251.

Contains an index of names.

1774–1775

Viola Root Cameron, *Emigrants from Scotland to America, 1774–1775. Copied from a Loose Bundle of Treasury Papers in the Public Record Office, London, England* (London, The Compiler 1930) 117 *f*   **21**

Only 100 typewritten copies made. Reissued in facsimile by the Genealogical Publishing Co, Baltimore, 1959.

Contains about 2,000 names and gives age, quality, occupation, former residence of each emigrant, and his reason for emigrating.

Lists of ships bound for the following destinations: New York, [1]–5; 28–29, 30–34, 35–36, 37–40, 54–55, 58–60, 61, 70–72, 73–75, 77–79; North Carolina, 6–24, 62, 72, 76 (Wilmington, 41–43, 45–46, 88–92), (Salem, 57); Pennsylvania (all bound for Philadelphia) 25–27, 44, 50–51, 67–69, 81–85; South Carolina, 76 (Charleston, 52); Georgia 61, 86 (Savannah, 47–49, 93–95).

See note for no 232.

1776–1803

Don Yoder, ed, "A New Emigrant List," *The Pennsylvania Dutchman* I (May 19 1949) 6   **22**

Appeared originally in German as an advertisement for missing heirs in the early Allentown weekly *Der Friedens-Bothe* for June 17 1825.

Contains the names of 32 emigrants who arrived in America during and after the Revolution.

No ship mentioned.

1800

Gerald Fothergill, "List of Emigrant Liverymen of London," *The New England Historical and Genealogical Register* LX (1906) 399–400   **23**

A short list giving only the name of the emigrant and the livery or guild to which he belonged.

No port of entry indicated and no ship mentioned.

1802–1850

See no 229.

1803–1806

Gerald Fothergill, "Passenger Lists to America," *The New England Historical and Genealogical Register* LX (1906) 23–28, 160–164, 240–243, 346–

All Ports, 1803–1806, continued

349; LXI (1907) 133–139, 265–270, 347–353; LXII (1908) 78–81, 168–171; LXVI (1912) 30–32, 306–308   **24**

Extensive lists of passengers leaving Ireland for America, 1803–1806. Copied from mss in the British Museum.

Includes ships to all parts of North America.

See notes for nos 25 and 26.

"Early Irish Emigrants to America, 1803–1806," *The Recorder; Bulletin of the American Irish Historical Society* III (June 1926) 19–23   **25**

Lists copied from mss in the British Museum. Gives name, age, occupation, and point of origin.

Contains lists of 3 ships destined for New York, 2 destined for New Castle and Philadelphia, and 1 for Philadelphia alone.

Additional material to no 24.

1804–1806

"American Passenger Lists, 1804–6 (British Musem Transcripts)" (*In* Ireland, Northern. Public Record Office *Report of the Deputy Keeper of the Records for the Year 1929*, Belfast, H. M. Stationery Office 1930, p 15, 21–49)   **26**

An alphabetical index of emigrants from counties Antrim, Armagh, Down, Fermanagh, Londonderry, and Tyrone sailing for New York, Philadelphia (or "Philadelphia and Newcastle"), Boston, Baltimore, Charleston, and New Bedford between June 1804 and Mar 1806.

Names interfiled in Appendix B, "Index to Documents (other than normal increments) deposited in the Public Record office during the year 1929," with only county of origin and year of departure specified.

Additional material to nos 24 and 25.

No ship mentioned.

1811

J. Dominick Hackett, "Passenger Lists Published in 'The Shamrock or Irish Chronicle,' 1811," *Journal of the American Irish Historical Society* XXVIII (1929–30) 65–82   **27**

List containing over 2,000 names transcribed and alphabetically arranged from individual lists in 1811 issues of *The Shamrock or Hibernian Chronicle,* a New York weekly published 1810–1817.

The individual ship lists previously printed in part in **27A** *The Recorder; Bulletin of the American Irish Historical Society,* Dec 1923, p 5–8; Nov 1924, p 11; Mar 1925, p 1–2; June 1926, p 2–19; Sept 1926, p 17–21; Dec 1926, p 23–32.

Lists passengers on 29 ships arriving at New York, 6 at Philadelphia, 1 at Baltimore, and 1 at New London.

See note for no 28.

1815–1816

Charles Montague Early, "Passenger Lists from 'The Shamrock or Irish Chronicle,' 1815–1816," *Journal of the American Irish Historical Society* XXIX (1930–31) 183–206   **28**

Supplementary material to no 27. Contains approximately 3,150 names.

Lists passengers on 60 ships arriving at New York, 11 at Philadelphia, and 1 at Baltimore.

1819–1820

United States. State Department, *Letter from the Secretary of State, with a Transcript of the List of Passengers Who Arrived in the United States from the 1st October, 1819, to the 30th September, 1820* (Washington, Gales & Seaton 1821) 288 p   **29**

16th Congress, 2d Session, Senate Document 118, Serial Number 45.

Contains 10,247 names arranged according to periodic returns by local Collectors of Customs. Includes ships to all parts of the United States.

Gives name, age, sex, occupation, and origin of each immigrant and the master and name of the ship in which he arrived.

MAINE

1602–1651

Wilbur D. Spencer, *Pioneers on Maine Rivers; with Lists to 1651, Compiled from the Original Sources* (Portland, Me, Lakeside Printing Co 1930) 414 p   *30*

A summary of the early European occupation of the coast of Maine and of the attempts at permanent settlement. Pages 13–23 contain "Maine Visiting Lists before 1630"; lists of "Pioneers," frequently with the name of the ships in which they arrived, follow chapters on the various river settlements.

NEW HAMPSHIRE

1631

"First Settlers of New Hampshire," *The New England Historical and Genealogical Register* II (1848) 37–39 **31**

Contains "The Names of Stewards and Servants sent by John Mason, Esq., into this Province of New Hampshire," p 39.

The date is only approximate.

Published previously with some slight variations in Nathaniel Adams, *Annals of Portsmouth* (Portsmouth 1825) p 18.

No ship mentioned.

1718

"The Petition to Governor Shute in 1718" (*In* Charles Knowles Bolton *Scotch Irish Pioneers in Ulster and America* (Boston, Bacon & Brown 1910, p 324–330) **32**

From a ms in the New Hampshire Historical Society, Concord.

Contains the names of over 250 inhabitants of Northern Ireland who in 1718 petitioned Samuel Shute, Governor of Massachusetts, for permission to transport themselves to New England. The names of many of these appear in the list of early settlers of Londonderry, N H, on p 262–264 of the book.

MASSACHUSETTS

1620

"Passengers of the Mayflower; the Names of Those Which Came Over First, in the Year 1620 and Were by the Blessing of God the First Beginers and (in a sort) the Foundation of All the Plantations and Colonies in New England; and Their Families" (*In* William Bradford *History of Plymouth Plantation*, 1620–1647, Boston, Massachusetts Historical Society 1912 II 397–412) **33**

There are several editions of Bradford's *History*, all of which have this list as an appendix. Of these, the ed of 1898 is the most easily obtainable on the out-of-print market.

Mayflower passenger lists are also printed in **33A** Nathaniel Bradstreet Shurtleff, "The Passengers of the May Flower in 1620," *The New England Historical and Genealogical Register* I (1847) 47–53; **33B** Algernon Aikin Aspinwall, "The Mayflower Passengers," *National Genealogical Society Quarterly* VI (1917) 56–57; **33C** Azel Ames, *The May-Flower and Her Log, July 15, 1620 – May 6, 1621, Chiefly from Original Sources* (Boston, Houghton, Mifflin & Co 1907) 166–195; **33D** "List of Passengers to America. From Authentic Sources," *The Genealogist's Note Book* I (1899) 66–67; **33E** "The Mayflower Series of Papers: 2," *The Historical Bulletin* IV (1904) 101–103; **33F** *List of Passengers Who Came to Plymouth in The "Mayflower" on Her First Trip in 1620* (New York, Society of Mayflower Descendants 1896); **33G** *Mayflower Descendants and Their Marriages* (Baltimore, Southern Book Co 1956).

1620–1623

Charles Edward Banks, *The English Ancestry and Homes of the Pilgrim Fathers Who Came to Plymouth on the "Mayflower" in 1620, the "Fortune" in 1621, and the "Anne" and the "Little James" in 1623* (New York, The Grafton Press 1929) 187 p **34**

Names of the various passengers, together with valuable information on their origin and later history, grouped alphabetically under the ship in which they arrived. Contains an appended list of the female passengers on the *Anne* and *Little James*.

Passenger lists of the *Anne* and *Fortune* may also be found in **34A** "The Mayflower Series of Papers: 5," *The Historical Bulletin* V (1904) 34–36. The lists of all four vessels also appear in: **34B** John A. Goodwin, *The Pilgrim Republic* (Boston, Ticknor and Co 1888; 2d ed, Boston and New York, Houghton Mifflin Co 1920) 183–186, 190–191, 242–244, 297–300; in **34C** Leon Clark Hills, *History and Genealogy of the Mayflower Planters and First Comers to Ye Olde Colonie* (Washington, Hills Publishing Co 1936) 20–22, 79–80, 84–86; and in **34D** an unidentified, 2-page pamphlet (n p, n d) which commences "List of Passengers in the Mayflower" and which has been pasted into a red-rope cover and bound into a pamphlet volume (IQH p v 34, no 14) in The New York Public Library.

Reissued in facsimile by the Genealogical Publishing Co, Baltimore, 1962.

1620–1640

Charles Edwards Banks, *The Planters of the Commonwealth; A Study of the Emigrants and Emigration in Colonial Times: To Which Are Added*

Massachusetts, 1620–1640, continued

Lists of Passengers to Boston and to the Bay Colony; the Ships Which Brought Them; Their English Homes, and the Places of Their Settlement in Massachusetts, 1620–1640 (Boston, Houghton, Mifflin Co 1930) 231 p
35

Lists 3600 passengers on 213 ships in chronological arrangement with indices of surnames and place names.

The most authoritative work covering this period. A reexamination of the original sources in the Public Record Office, London, and comprising the collection of Custom House records of English ports, already accomplished in part by Savage, no 47; Drake, no 44; and Hotten, no 1.

Reissued in facsimile by the Genealogical Publishing Co, Baltimore, 1961.

1621–1769

George Francis Donovan, *The Pre-Revolutionary Irish in Massachusetts, 1620–1775* (Menasha, Wis, George Banta Pub Co 1932) 158 p   **36**

Irish immigrants between 1621 and 1769, but mostly between 1753 and 1769. For a number of passenger lists of ships arriving between these dates see p 30–40.

Only names of Irish origin are given, extracted almost entirely from no 64.

Doctoral dissertation, St Louis University 1931.

1629

"Passengers on the Mayflower 1629" (*In* Leon Clark Hills *History and Genealogy of the Mayflower Planters and First Comers to Ye Olde Colonie,* Washington, Hills Publishing Co 1936, i 86)   **37**

Contains the names of 23 of the 35 passengers who sailed from Gravesend, London, Mar 1629 and arrived at Plymouth May 15 1629.

1629–1635

John G. Locke, "Emigrants in Vessels, 'Bound to Virginia'," *The New England Historical and Genealogical Register* v (1851) 248–249   **38**

A general article showing that some passengers in vessels "bound for Virginia" did in fact emigrate to Massachusetts. Gives the names of a number of emigrants who eventually settled in Massachusetts and the ships in which they arrived.

1630

Charles Edward Banks, *The Winthrop Fleet of 1630; an Account of the Vessels, the Voyage, the Passengers and Their English Homes from Original Authorities* (Boston, Houghton Mifflin Co 1930) 118 p   **39**

Excellent background material on the early emigrants, giving details of preparations, voyage, origins, etc.

Over 700 names alphabetically arranged. Contains also an alphabetical list of the 40 heads of families on the *Mary and John*, which sailed contemporaneously with the Winthrop Fleet.

A short list of the "Leaders in the Winthrop Fleet, 1630," can be found in *The New England Historical and Genealogical Register* LXXV (1921) 236–237. "Believed" and "conjectural" passengers of the flag-ship *Arabella* [*Arbella*] are given in no 40. Reissued in facsimile by the Genealogical Publishing Co, Baltimore, 1961.

Albert R. Rogers, *The Historic Voyage of the Arbella, 1630; Official Souvenir of the Arbella, on Exhibition, Charles River Basin, Boston, 1930, under the Auspices of the Massachusetts Bay Tercentenary, Inc.* (Boston, Arbella Co [1930]) 32 p   **40**

"Believed Passengers in the Arbella," p 15; "Conjectural Passengers," p 17. See no 39.

Maude Pinney Kuhns, *The "Mary and John"; a Story of the Founding of Dorchester, Massachusetts, 1630* (Rutland, Vt, Tuttle Publishing Co 1943) 254 p   **41**

A reconstructed list of passengers who sailed from Plymouth, England, on the *Mary and John* Mar 20 1630. Contains genealogical accounts of all passengers and their descendents.

1630–1641

"Time of the Arrival in New England of the Following Ministers," *The New England Historical and Genealogical Register* I (1847) 289   **42**

Sixty-five names listed under year of arrival.
No ship mentioned.

1630–1662

John Farmer, *A Genealogical Register of the First Settlers of New-England; Containing an Alphabetical List of the Governours, Deputy-Governours, Assistants or Counsellors, and Ministers of the Gospel in the Several Colonies, from 1620 to 1692; Representatives of the General Court of Massachusetts, from 1634 to 1692; Graduates of Harvard College to 1662; Members of the Ancient and Honourable Artillery Company to 1662; Freemen Admitted to the Massachusetts Colony from 1630 to 1662; with Many Other of the Early Inhabitants of New-England and Long-Island, N. Y., from 1620 to the Year 1675: To Which Are Added Various Genealogical and Biographical Notes, Collected from Ancient Records, Manuscripts, and Printed Works* (Lancaster, Mass: Carter, Andrews, & Co 1829) 352 p   **43**

Contains "the freemen admitted to the Massachusetts colony from 1630–1662 and the names of all such emigrants, both freemen and non-freemen, as could be collected, who had come over to the several colonies before 1643."

An invaluable directory to the first settlers of New England and listing, as it does, the emigrants between 1630 and 1643 among the others worthy of inclusion here.

See 43A Samuel G. Drake, "A List of Names Found Among the First Settlers of New England," *The New England Historical and Genealogical Register* I (1847) 137–139, for additions and corrections.

No ship mentioned.

1631–1671

Samuel G. Drake, *Result of Some Researches among the British Archives for Information Relative to The Founders of New England: Made in the Years 1858, 1859, and 1860. Originally Collected for and Published in the New England Historical and Genealogical Register, and Now Corrected and Enlarged* (Boston, New England Historical and Genealogical Register 1860) 143 p   **44**

A collection of emigrant lists to New England covering principally the years 1634–1635 but containing some items between 1631–1671.

Has indices of passengers, persons, places, and ships.

Printed also in part and with some variation in **44A** "The Founders of New England," *The New England Historical and Genealogical Register* xiv (1860) 297–359. A 3d ed **44B** of which "seventy-five copies in quarto [were] privately reprinted by permission of Mr. Drake for W. Elliot Woodward," was issued from the press of John Wilson and Son, Boston, 1865. Paging here identical with the present item, but the 3d ed contains an additional section, "The First Settlers of Plymouth." Ship names in this appended matter appear in the analytical index.

See note for no 35.

Reissued in facsimile by the Genealogical Publishing Co, Baltimore.

1634

"Passengers of the Mary and John, 1634," *The New England Historical and Genealogical Register* ix (1855) 265–268   **45**

Includes also a partial list of the *Hercules*, 1634.

1634–1637

Eben Putnam, "Two Early Passenger Lists, 1635–1637," *The New England Historical and Genealogical Register* lxxv (1921) 217–226   **46**

Passengers on the *Hercules* of Sandwich.

See *The New England Historical and Genealogical Register* lxxix (1925) 107–109 for additions and corrections.

Printed in part in **46A** William Boys, *Collections for an History of Sandwich in Kent* (Canterbury 1792 p 751); in **46B** James Savage, "Gleanings for New England History," *Collections of the Massachusetts Historical Society* 3d ser iii (1843) 274–275; and in **46C** "Emigrants in the Hercules of Sandwich," *The New England Historical and Genealogical Register* xv (1861) 28–29.

1634–1638

James Savage, "Gleanings for New England History," *Collections of The Massachusetts Historical Society* 3d ser viii (1843) 243–348; 3d ser x (1849) 127–146   **47**

Contains a great many lists of early emigrants to New England copied from original records in Rolls Court, Westminster Hall, London.
See note for no 35.

1635

William S. Appleton, "More Passengers for New-England," *The New England Historical and Genealogical Register* xxv (1871) 13–15 **48**
From mss in the Public Record Office, London.
Passengers from Weymouth March 20 1635.
No ship mentioned.

"A List of Suche Passeng^rs as Shipt Themselves at the Towne of Hampton in the James of London of iije Tonnes William Coop^r Mr, — V^rs New England in and about V^t of April 1635" (*In* Louise Brownell Clarke *The Greenes of Rhode Island, with Historical Records of English Ancestry, 1534–1902; Compiled from the MSS. of the Late Major-General George Sears Greene, U. S. V.* New York, The Knickerbocker Press 1903, p 769) **49**
Extracted from the "Colonial Documents," v 8, fol 67, in the Public Record Office, London.
Contains 51 names.

Annie Haven Thwing, "The following persons embarked for New England in the 'Susan and Ellen,' April, 1635. . . ," *The New England Historical and Genealogical Register* lv (1901) 345 **50**
The names and ages of 24 passengers on the *Susan and Ellen*, 1635.

1637–1639

Charles Boardman Jewson, *Transcript of Three Registers of Passengers from Great Yarmouth to Holland and New England, 1637–1639* (Norwich, Norfolk Record Society 1954) 98 p **51**
Volume xxv of *Norfolk Record Society Publications*.
Transcribed from one document in the Bodleian Library and two in the Public Record Office.
Arranged chronologically. Entries include name, domicile, birthplace, occupation or quality, age, destination, reason for journey, and anticipated date of return.
Contains indices of persons, occupations and qualities, and places.
Emigrants destined for New England previously included in no 1.
No ship mentioned.

1638

Henry Stevens, "Passengers for New England, 1638," *The New England Historical and Genealogical Register* ii (1848) 108–110 **52**
A list of 110 passengers on the *Confidence* of London, April 11 1638.
See *The New England Historical and Genealogical Register* v (1851) 440 for corrections.
Also printed in corrected form in nos 35 and 44.

Massachusetts, continued

1651–1652

"Scotch Prisoners Sent to Massachusetts in 1652, by Order of the English Government," *The New England Historical and Genealogical Register* I (1847) 377–380   53

List of passengers aboard the *John and Sarah* of London November 1651 – May 1652.

Also printed alphabetically arranged in   53A Charles Edward Banks, "Scotch Prisoners Deported to New England by Cromwell, 1651–52," *Massachusetts Historical Society Proceedings* LXI (1928) 4–29, together with the names of a number of prisoners who eventually settled at Lynn and Kittery (now Berwick).

1656

"A Lyst of the Pasingers Abord the Speedwell of London, Robert Lock Master, Bound for New England," *The New England Historical and Genealogical Register* I (1847) 132   54

List of 41 persons who landed at Boston May 27 1656.

Printed also in no 44, p 77, and in   54A John Cox, Jr, "Notes on the Eight Names Marked as Quakers in the Speedwell List, 1656," *The New York Genealogical and Biographical Record* LXV (1934) 45–47, where a photostat illustration of the original ms in the Pierpont Morgan Library appears.

1657–1686

Gordon Ireland, "Servants to Foreign Plantations from Bristol, England, to New England, 1657–1686," *The New England Historical and Genealogical Register* XCIII (1939) 381–388   55

An extract from no 11 of servants destined for New England during the period covered.

Names arranged chronologically, with name of person to whom bound, date of entry, and reference to location in "Servants to Foreign Plantations," the ms source volume.

Main list followed by table of bond-masters and table of ships.

1660–1684

J. Henry Lea, "Genealogical Gleanings among the English Archives," *The New England Historical and Genealogical Register* LV (1901) 331–339 56

References to New England families in Bristol apprentice books now preserved at the Council House in Bristol. Entries cover the period 1660–1684.

1662–1763

"Passengers to America," *The New England Historical and Genealogical Register* XXX (1876) 39–43, 459–461; XXXI (1877) 309–312; XXXII (1878) 407–411; XXXIII (1879) 307–310; XXXVII (1883) 162–163   57

A miscellaneous collection of ship arrivals, passenger lists, passenger arrivals culled from court records, etc, gathered together mostly from mss belonging to the "New-England Historic, Genealogical Society."

In 12 numbers or sections: no 2 contributed by Arthur M. Alger, Boston; nos 4, 9–11 contributed by Henry F. Waters, Boston; no 5 contributed by John S. H. Fogg, South Boston.

Later parts titled "Passengers and Vessels That Have Arrived in America."

1670

Henry F. Waters, "Passengers to New-England in 1670," *The New England Historical and Genealogical Register* xxviii (1874) 447   **58**

From the court files of Essex County, Massachusetts.

A receipt for the passage of several persons in the *Happy Return* from Plymouth, England, to Boston, 1670.

1671

"Passengers for New England," *The New England Historical and Genealogical Register* ii (1848) 407   **59**

A list of the passengers on board the *Arabella* bound for New England May 27 1671.

1679

Henry F. Waters, "More Passengers to New-England, 1679," *The New England Historical and Genealogical Register* xxviii (1874) 375–378   **60**

Extracted from Essex County Court papers and a book of notorial records in the Clerk's Office, County of Essex, Massachusetts.

Passengers of the *Hannah and Elizabeth* and the *Nathaniel* of Dartmouth.

List of the *Hannah and Elizabeth* also printed in   **60A** "Passengers for New England," *The Essex Antiquarian* iv (1900) 137.

1685

Colin Campbell, "Deportations from Scotland in 1685," *The New England Historical and Genealogical Register* cxiv (1960) 150–151   **61**

From a document in the Scottish Record Office, H. M. Register House, Edinburgh.

A petition by a Scotch merchant-owner of a ship bound for New England for a number of prisoners captured in the unsuccessful rising of the Earl of Argyll in the spring of 1685, with the names of 15 prisoners granted to him for transportation overseas.

1687

"Passengers for New England," *The Essex Antiquarian* xi (1907) 65   **62**

From Essex Registry of Deeds.

Copy of document signed by four emigrants before leaving London.

No ship mentioned.

Massachusetts, continued

1700–1775

Ethel Stanwood Bolton, *Immigrants to New England, 1700–1775* (Salem, Mass, The Essex Institute 1931) 235 p   **63**

Not original lists, but an alphabetical list of persons coming to New England during the period covered with reference to where found.

Contains an index of all names mentioned in the volume.

Reprinted from   **63A** *The Essex Institute Historical Collections* LXIII (1927) 177–192, 269–284, 365–380; LXIV (1928) 25–32, 257–272; LXV (1929) 57–72, 113–128, 531–546; LXVI (1930) 411–426, 521–536; LXVII (1931) 89–112, 201–224, 305–328.

1714–1769

Boston. Registry Department, *A Volume of Records Relating to the Early History of Boston Containing Miscellaneous Papers* (Boston, Municipal Printing Office 1900) 389 p   **64**

From a volume of records in the City Clerk's Office, Boston.

Document No 100–1900. Twenty-ninth in a series of reports issued under the direction of the Record Commissioners, Boston.

Port arrivals and immigrant lists appear on p 229–332.

Contains an index to all surnames in the volume.

See notes for nos 36 and 65.

1716–1766

"Various Sailings from Scotland to Boston between 1716 and 1766," *The Scottish Genealogist* VII (1960) 14–15   **65**

"From The Commissioners' Reports, Boston Records, vol. 29, doc. 100 in the Mass. Hist. Association, Boston, Mass., U. S.A." Contains short lists for 8 voyages.

Extracts from no 64.

1716–1769

Michael J. O'Brien, "Irish Immigrants to New England: Extracts from the Minutes of the Selectmen of the Town of Boston, Mass.," *The Journal of the American Irish Historical Society* XIII (1914) 177–187   **66**

Irish immigrants between 1716 and 1769, but mostly between 1762 and 1769.

1798–1800

Mrs Georgie A. Hill, "Passenger Arrivals at Salem and Beverly, Mass., 1798–1800; With an Introduction by Meredith B. Colket, Jr., of Washington, D. C.," *The New England Historical and Genealogical Register* CVI (1952) 203–209   **67**

Copied from customs records in the National Archives, Washington.

Arranged chronologically.

RHODE ISLAND

1636

John Farmer, "First Settlers of Rhode Island," *New England Historical and Genealogical Register* i (1847) 91   **68**

Contains 93 names; no ship mentioned.

1686

Elisha R. Potter, *Memoir Concerning the French Settlements and French Settlers in the Colony of Rhode Island* (Providence, Sidney S. Rider 1879) 138 p   **69**

Number 5 of *Rhode Island Historical Tracts*.

Contains the names, with genealogical notes and other data, of a band of French emigrants who in 1686 made an agreement for the settlement of a plantation in Narragansett County.

No ship mentioned.

1701–1766

Sidney S. Rider, *The History of Denization and Naturalization in the Colony of Rhode Island, 1636–1790* (n p, 1905?) 14 p   **70**

A general account of the Rhode Island law of naturalization before the adoption by Rhode Island of the Constitution of the United States in 1790.

Contains the names of approximately a dozen foreigners naturalized between 1701–1766, as shown by court records and statutes of the General Assembly.

No ship mentioned.

CONNECTICUT

1637–1638

[Passengers on the *Hector*, 1637–1638] (*In* Isabel MacBeath Calder *The New Haven Colony,* New Haven, Yale University Press 1934, p 29–31)
71

Includes the names of a number of passengers accompanying John Davenport and Theophilus Eaton to Connecticut (*via* Boston), 1637–1638.

1811

See no 27.

NEW YORK

1600–1700

Joel N. Eno, "New York 'Knickerbocker' Families; Origin and Settlement," *The New York Genealogical and Biographical Record* xlv (1914) 387–391
72

A list of Dutch immigrants to New York during the seventeenth century, giving place of origin in Holland and settlement in North America.
No ship mentioned.

1610–1664

"Deutsche Einzeleinwanderer und Familien in Neu-Niederland," *Jahrbuch für Auslanddeutsche Sippenkunde* i (1936) 45–53
73

Appended to an article on p 44–45 by Otto Lohr entitled "Amerikadeutsche Familien des 17. Jahrhunderts."
Gives names of German individuals and families in New York during the period covered, with place of origin frequently indicated.
No ship mentioned.

1620–1664

Richard Schermerhorn, Jr, "Representative Pioneer Settlers of New Netherland and Their Original Home Places," *The New York Genealogical and Biographical Record* lxv (1934) 2–12
74

An alphabetical list of New Netherland settlers, 1620–1664, with their original places of residence in Holland, Belgium and Germany.
Contains a table of localities from which they came.
No ship mentioned.

1630–1646

"Name of Settlers in Rensselaerswyck from 1630 to 1646; Compiled from the Books of Monthly Wages and Other MSS." (*In* Edmund Bailey O'Callaghan *History of New Netherland; or, New York under the Dutch*, New York, D. Appleton & Co 1846, i 433–441)
75

Settlers listed chronologically, with brief sketches of their immigration and later lives given when known.
Also printed in **75A** "Settlers in Rensselaerswyck from 1630 to 1646, Compiled from the Books of Monthly Wages and Other mss," *Year Book of The Holland Society of New York* (1896) 130–140.
See note for no 76.

1630–1658

"Settlers of Rensselaerswyck, 1630–1658" (*In* Arnold Johan Ferdinand Van Laer *Van Rensselaer Bowier Manuscripts, Being the Letters of Kiliaen Van Rensselaer, 1630–1643, and Other Documents Relating to the Colony of Rensselaerswyck*, Albany, University of the State of New York 1908, p 805–846)
76

New York, 1630–1658, continued

New York State Library Bulletin, History, Number 7.
A record of the arrival of settlers in the colony from the date of its founding to the end of the administration of Jan Baptist Van Rensselaer.
Much more comprehensive and covering a longer period than item no 75, giving places of origin, occupations, and the names of the ships in which most of the settlers arrived.
See note for no 80.

1630–1674

John O. Evjen, *Scandinavian Immigrants in New York, 1630–1674. With Appendices on Scandinavians in Mexico and South America, 1532–1640, Scandinavians in Canada, 1619–1620, Some Scandinavians in New York in the Eighteenth Century, German Immigrants in New York, 1630–1674* (Minneapolis, K. C. Holter Pub Co 1916) 438 p   **77**

A collection of biographic articles on Norwegian, Danish, and Swedish immigrants who settled in New York during the period covered.

1633–1644

"Secretary van Tienhoven's Answer to the Remonstrance from New Netherland" (*In* Edmund Bailey O'Callaghan *Documents Relative to the Colonial History of the State of New York,* Albany, Weed, Parsons & Co 1856, I 422–432)   **78**

From the ms in the Royal Archives at the Hague.
The defence by Cornelius van Tienhoven of the existing system of government in New Netherland, 1650. Contains the names of 11 colonists who signed the Remonstrance and gives a brief account of their activities in the colony, including the dates of their arrival and the ships in which they came.
Also printed in   **78A** "Van Tienhoven's Answer to the Vertoogh," *Collections of the New-York Historical Society* 2d ser II (1849) 329–338; and in   **78B** "Answer to the Representation of New Netherland, by Cornelius von Tienhoven, 1650," *in* J. Franklin Jameson, ed, *Narratives of New Netherland, 1609–1664,* New York, Charles Scribner's Sons 1909, p 359–377.

1636–1642

"Lijst van Eenige Koloniers door Kiliaen Van Rensselaer in de Jaren 1636–1642 uit het Vaderland naar Zijne Kolonie Gezonden," *Oud-Holland* VIII (1890) 296   **79**

Contains the names of 29 colonists accompanying Kiliaen Van Rensselaer, 1636–1642, with their places of origin and occupations given.
No ship mentioned.

1637

Arnold Johan Ferdinand Van Laer, "Settlers of the Colony of Rensselaerswyck," *The New York Genealogical and Biographical Record* XLIX (1918) 365–367   *80*

From a Rensselaerswyck ms now in the New York State Library, Albany.

A list of emigrants indebted to the owners of the ship *Rensselaerswyck* for board beginning 1 Oct 1636 and ending 1637 on the date when each person landed in New Netherland. Contains 33 names of men, women and children and gives the exact date when each person left the ship.

Also printed in no 76.

1639

"Form of Oath Taken by the Englishmen on and about Manhattan Island with Their Signatures" (*In* Berthold Fernow *Documents Relating to the History of the Early Colonial Settlements Principally on Long Island, with a Map of Its Western Part, Made in 1666,* Albany, Weed, Parsons & Co 1883, p 24–25)   **81**

Old series vol xiv (new series vol iii) of *Documents Relating to the Colonial History of the State of New York.*

The names of 8 Englishmen who subscribed to an oath of allegiance to the Dutch government and to the colony of New Netherland, Aug 1639.

1639–1663

William J. Hoffman, "Random Notes Concerning Settlers of Dutch Descent," *The American Genealogist* xxix (1953) 65–76, 146–152; xxx (1954) 38–44   **82**

Biographical and genealogical notes on servants and employees hired in New Netherland during the period covered.

xxx 38–44 contains a tabular résumé of the persons noticed, giving the year each was engaged for employment, his age at the time, his place of origin, the purpose of his employment (occupation), and his employer. All such persons listed were of foreign origin.

1654–1664

"List of Passengers, 1654 to 1664," *Year Book of The Holland Society of New York* (1902) 5–37   **83**

A more complete, accurate, and time-inclusive list than no 86, giving Dutch and English form of ship's name and origin of immigrant.

Contains indices of passengers and places of origin.

From New York Colonial mss xiii 75, 88, 106 xiv, 83–123.

Additional information from James Riker's copy of same original source (in Manuscript Division, The New York Public Library) was published by Rosalie Fellows Bailey in *The New York Genealogical and Biographical Record* for October 1963.

Van Brunt Bergen, "A List of Early Immigrants to New Netherland; Alphabetically Arranged, with Additions and Corrections, from Manuscripts of the Late Teunis G. Bergen," *The New York Genealogical and Biographical Record* xiv (1883) 181–190; xv (1884) 34–40, 72–77   **84**

An alphabetical arrangement of the combined lists of nos 75, 86, and 88.

Coded to designate the ship in which each immigrant arrived.

New York, continued

1655

"Letter from the Burgomasters of Amsterdam to Stuyvesant: Boys and Girls from the Almhouses Sent to New Netherland" (*In* Berthold Fernow *Documents Relating to the History of the Early Colonial Settlements Principally on Long Island, with a Map of Its Western Part, Made in 1666,* Albany, Weed, Parsons & Co 1883, p 325–326)   **85**

Old series vol xiv (new series vol iii) of *Documents Relating to the Colonial History of the State of New York.*

Contains the names and ages of 17 children sent from the almshouses of Amsterdam to New Amsterdam, 1655.

No ship mentioned.

1657–1664

"Early Immigrants to New Netherland; 1657–1667" (*In* Edmund Bailey O'Callaghan *The Documentary History of the State of New-York*, Albany, Secretary of State 1850, iii 33–42)   **86**

Ship lists arranged chronologically, with immigrants names only.

Also printed in   **86A** "Passenger Lists 1657 to 1664," *Year Book of The Holland Society of New York* (1896) 141–158.

See note for no 83.

1678

Kenneth E. Hasbrouck, "The Huguenots of New Paltz, N. Y.," *De Halve Maen* xxxvi (Jan 1962) 7–8, 12, 15   **87**

Contains the names of the 12 Huguenot patentees who founded the Ulster County community of New Paltz in 1678, and gives the dates and places of their births and dates of their removal from the Palatinate.

Also printed with genealogical notes in   **87A** Ralph LeFevre, *History of New Paltz, New York, and Its Old Families (from 1678 to 1820)*, Albany, Fort Orange Press 1903, 2d ed 1909, p 13, 16 (facsimile of their signatures), 505–530.

See also no 199.

1683–1684

See no 12.

1687

"The Roll off Those Who Haue Taken the Oath off Allegiance in the Kings County in the Province of New Yorke the 26: 27: 28: 29: and 30th Day off September In the Third Yeare of His May^tsh Raigne Annoq^ue Domine 1687" (*In* Edmund Bailey O'Callaghan *The Documentary History of the State of New-York*, Albany, Secretary of State 1850, i 429–432)   **88**

From a ms in the office of the Secretary of State.

Contains name and age only.

Also printed in   **88A** *Year Book of the Holland Society of New York* (1896) 159–166.

1687–1776

Morgan H. Seacord, *Biographical Sketches and Index of the Huguenot Settlers of New Rochelle*, 1687–1776 (New Rochelle, N Y, The Huguenot and Historical Association of New Rochelle 1941) 54 p **89**

An alphabetical list of Huguenot emigrants who settled in New Rochelle before the Revolution. Entries include time and place of birth, ancestry, time of arrival and marriage and death of each settler.

No ship mentioned.

1708

"The Kocherthal Party — the 1708 Immigration to New York" (*In* Walter Allen Knittle *Early Eighteenth Century Palatine Emigration*, Philadelphia, Dorrance & Co 1937, p 243–244) **90**

Fifty-three Palatines coming to Newburgh, N Y, under the leadership of Reverend Kocherthal.

Also printed in **90A** "London Documents: The Names, Trades, Etc., of the German Protestants to be Settled in New York," in Lou D. MacWethy, *The Book of Names*. St Johnsville, N Y, The Enterprise and News 1933, p 51–52; in **90B** "Names and Occupations of Newburgh Palatines," *Olde Ulster; an Historical and Genealogical Magazine* IX (1913) 102–103; and in **90C** "The Names, Trades, &c., of the German Protestants to be Settled at New-York," in Edmund Bailey O'Callaghan, *Documents Relative to the Colonial History of New-York*, Albany, Weed, Parsons & Co 1855, v 52–53. Also printed in no 144.

1709

"Lists of Germans from the Palatinate Who Came to England in 1709," *The New York Genealogical and Biographical Record* XL (1909) 49–54, 93–100, 160–167, 241–248; XLI (1910) 10–19 **91**

Four Board of Trade lists of the first 6520 Palatines to arrive that year, compiled in England by John Tribbeko and George Ruperti, the German ministers. Many of these came shortly thereafter to America.

Names grouped under occupations, with age of head of household, the notation "wife" or "sing," the ages of sons and daughters, and church affiliation.

The first of these lists is printed in **91A** "The Board of Trade List of the First Party of Palatines in London, May 3, 1709," *in* Walter Allen Knittle, *Early Eighteenth Century Palatine Emigration* (Philadelphia, Dorrance & Co 1937) p 244–247, and the entire lists appear in no 92 in alphabetical order but in a somewhat abridged form.

See note for no 93.

"List of Palatines in 1709" (*In* Lou D. MacWethy *The Book of Names,* St Johnsville, N Y, The Enterprise and News 1933, p 75–111) **92**

Contains the four London lists of Palatines from Germany, May 1 – June 11 1709 (see nos 91 and 93), each arranged in separate alphabetical order. Gives name only.

"The Embarkation Lists from Holland" (*In* Walter Allen Knittle *Early Eighteenth Century Palatine Emigration*, Philadelphia, Dorrance & Co 1937, p 248–274) **93**

New York, 1709, continued

Lists of five separate sailings of some 11,000 persons from Holland to England compiled in Rotterdam and forwarded to England. Many of these Palatines came shortly thereafter to America.

Supplementary to nos 91 and 92.

Ulrich Simmendinger, *True and Authentic Register of Persons Still Living, by God's Grace, Who in the Year 1709, under the Wonderful Providences of the Lord Journeyed from Germany to America or New World and There Seek Their Piece of Bread at Various Places. Reported with Joy to All Admirers, Especially to Their Families and Close Friends by Ulrich Simmendinger, a North American, Seven Years in the Providence of New York but Now Returned to his Native City, Reutlingen. Printed there by John G. Feusing. Translated from the German by Herman F. Vesper* (St Johnsville, N Y, The Enterprise and News 1934) 20 p   **94**

Published originally as *Warhoffte und Glaubwürdige Verzeichnis Jeniger Personen; Welche Sich Anno 1709 aus Teutschland in Americam oder Neue Welt Begeben . . .* (Reutlingen ca 1717).

Also printed in   **94A** "The Simmendinger Register," *in* Walter Allen Knittle, *Early Eighteenth Century Palatine Emigration*, Philadelphia, Dorrance & Co 1937, p 291–299.

Reissued in facsimile by the Genealogical Publishing Co, Baltimore, 1962.

1710

"List of the Palatins Remaining at New York, 1710" (*In* Edmund Bailey O'Callaghan *The Documentary History of the State of New-York*, Albany, Secretary of State 1850, III 339–341)   **95**

A census of newly-arrived immigrants remaining in New York.

Gives name and age of head of household and names and ages of his wife and children.

Also printed in   **95A** "List of the Palatines Remaining at New York, 1710," *in* Lou D. MacWethy, *The Book of Names*, St Johnsville, N Y, The Enterprise and News 1933, p 120–123. Also printed in no 144.

"Statement of Heads of Palaten Fameleys and Number of Persons in Both Towns on ye West Side of Hudsons River. Winter, 1710" (*In* Edmund Bailey O'Callaghan *The Documentary History of the State of New York*, Albany, Secretary of State 1850, III 343)   **96**

A census of newly-arrived Palatines living in the "west camp," 1710.

Gives name of head of household and number of dependents.

Also printed in   **96A** "West Camp; Statement of Heads of Palaten Fameleys and Number of Persons in Both Towns of ye West Side Hudsons River. Winter, 1710," *in* Lou D. MacWethy, *The Book of Names*, St Johnsville, N Y, The Enterprise and News 1933, p 123–124.

1710–1712

"The New York Subsistence List" (*In* Walter Allen Knittle *Early Eighteenth Century Palatine Emigration*, Philadelphia, Dorrance & Co 1937, p 282–291)   **97**

Alphabetical list of 847 debtors to the British government for subsistence given either in New York City or Hudson River settlements from their landing in 1710 to Sept 1712.

From a ms "journal" in the Public Record Office, London.

Also printed in **97A** "Palatine Heads of Families from Governor Hunter's Ration Lists, June, 1710 to September, 1714," *in* Lou D. MacWethy, *The Book of Names*, St Johnsville, N Y, The Enterprise and News, 1933, p 65–72.

1710–1714

"Names of the Palatine Children Apprenticed by Gov. Hunter 1710–1714" (*In* Edmund Bailey O'Callaghan *The Documentary History of the State of New-York*, New York, Secretary of State 1850, III 341–342)   **98**

Names of orphan and destitute Palatine children apprenticed for training and care, 1710–1714.

Gives name of child, his age, parents, the person to whom he was bound, and that person's locality.

Also printed in **98A** "Names of the Palatine Children Apprenticed by Gov. Hunter, 1710–1714," in Lou D. MacWethy, *The Book of Names*, St Johnsville, N Y, The Enterprise and News 1933, p 128–129. Also printed in no 144.

1715–1716

"The Oath of Abjuration, 1715–1716," *The New-York Historical Society Quarterly Bulletin* III (1919) 35–40   **98-1**

From the original preserved among the archives of The New-York Historical Society.

A chronological record kept by Mayor's Court of the City of New York of the names of 125 foreigners who were naturalized under an act passed by the General Assembly in July 1715. Gives name only.

1715–1773

Lyle Frederick Bellinger, "Our Early Citizens: Names of Those Taking the Oath of Allegiance from 1715 to 1773" (*In* Lou D. MacWethy *The Book of Names*, St Johnsville, N Y, The Enterprise and News 1933, p 1–7)   **99**

Lists of Palatine naturalizations, compiled from Colonial Laws of New York, from Munsell's *Annals of Albany*, etc.

1736–1742

Edmund Bailey O'Callaghan, "Early Highland Immigration to New York," *The Historical Magazine and Notes and Queries Concerning the Antiquities, History and Biography of America* 1 ser, v (1861) 301–304   **100**

A list of the Scotch Highlanders led by Captain Lauchlin Campbell in 1736, and of other later parties.

No ship mentioned.

See note for no 101.

1738–1742

"The Argyle Patent and Accompanying Documents" (*In* Jennie M. Patten *History of the Somonauk Presbyterian Church near Sandwich, DeKalb*

New York, 1738–1742, continued

County, Illinois, with Ancestral Lines of the Early Members, Chicago, Privately Printed for James A. Patten and Henry J. Patten 1928, p 297–346)											**101**

Includes 4 lists of immigrants, as follows: "A List of ffamilies from the Island of North Britane" who unsuccessfully petitioned for a grant of land in Albany County in Oct 1738, p 298–299; "A List of the Persons Brought from Scotland by Captain Lauchlin Campbell to settle the Kings Lands at the Wood Creek from 1738 to 1740," p 326–329; "List of Persons brought from Scotland by Capt. Laughlin Campbell in 1738–40," p 329–335; and "A further Account Delivered by Alexander McNaught[on] and Duncan Reid of Persons who did Emigrate with Captain Campbell in 1738, 1739, and 1740 . . . ," p 336–338.

Also printed in part in no 100.

No ship mentioned.

1738–1750

See no 17–1.

1740–1769

Richard J. Wolfe, "The Colonial Naturalization Act of 1740; With a List of Persons Naturalized in New York Colony, 1740–1769," *The New York Genealogical and Biographical Record* xciv (1963) 132–147			**102**

From a ms in The New York Public Library.

Contains the names of approximately 300 persons naturalized in New York Colony during the period covered.

A more complete and comprehensive record of New York Naturalizations than that contained in no 19, where an imperfect copy of the present list was used as a source.

The names of Jews in the present list were previously extracted and published in Leon Hühner, "Naturalization of Jews in New York under the Act of 1740," *Publications of the American Jewish Historical Society* xiii (1905) 1–6.

1774

"Journal of Colonel Alexander Harvey of Scotland and Barnet, Vermont," *Proceedings of the Vermont Historical Society* (1921–1923) 199–262												**102–1**

P 204 contains the names of the seamen and a company of farmers with Colonel Alexander Harvey on a journey from Scotland to New York on the Brigantine *Matty*, Captain Thomas Chochran, Master, May 19 – July 22 1774. The company later settled in Barnet, Vermont.

Also printed in **102–1A** Frederic Palmer Wells, *History of Barnet, Vermont, from the Outbreak of the French and Indian War to Present Time* (Burlington, Free Press Printing Co 1923) p 23.

1774–1775

Wallace R. Freeman, "Scotch Emigrants to New York 1774–1775," *The Niagara Frontier Genealogical Magazine* iv (1944) 89–90, 124–125, 136–137, 145												**103**

Lists of Scotch emigrants who shipped from Stanaer on May 16 1774 in the *Gale* and on July 9 1775 in the *Commerce*.
Extracted from no 21.

1789–1855

"Aliens Authorized to Purchase and Hold Real Estate in this State" (*In* Henry H. Havens *General Index to the Laws of the State of New York*, Albany, Weed, Parsons & Co 1866, I [1777–1857 inclusive] 31–73)   **104**

A list of alien residents of New York State granted statutory right to buy and hold real estate as any natural born citizen could do. Covers the period 1789–1855, but most such statutes were enacted within the years 1789–1828.
Gives name and reference to statute only.

1802–1814

Richard J. Wolfe, "Early New York Naturalization Records in the Emmet Collection; with a List of Aliens Naturalized in New York 1802–1814," *Bulletin of The New York Public Library* LXVII (1963) 211–217   **105**

Contains the names of 115 aliens, mostly Irish, naturalized in New York during the period covered. Gives name, place of birth, age, allegience, country from which the alien emigrated, place of intended settlement, and date.

1803–1806

See no 25.

1811

See no 27.

1815–1816

See no 28.

1820

[Passenger manifest of the ship *Manhattan*, 1820] Printed below, p 38–39.
106

Contains the names of 18 passengers who landed at New York on Aug 18 1820.
From a ms in The New York Public Library.

1825

Rasmus B. Anderson, "'Restaurationen' — the Norse Mayflower," *The American Scandinavian Review* XIII (1925) 348–360   **107**

Names and biographies of 53 passengers who sailed from Stavanger for New York July 5 1825. Made up from memories of surviving members.
Also printed in **107A** Rasmus B. Anderson, *The First Chapter of Norwegian Immigration, (1821–1840) Its Causes and Results* (Madison, Wis 1896) p 91–93; and in **107B** Theodore Blegen, *Norwegian Migration to America, 1825–1860* (Northfield, Minn 1931) I 395–396.

DISTRICT OF NEW-YORK.—PORT OF NEW-YORK.

I _Dexter Parr Jr._ do solemnly, sincerely and truly _swear_ that the following List or Manifest of Passengers, subscribed with my name, and now delivered by me to the Collector of the Customs for the District of New-York, contains to the best of my knowledge and belief a just and true account of all the Passengers received on board the _Ship Manhattan_ whereof I am Master, from _Liverpool_ — _So help me God._

Sworn to, the 8 _Aug_ ———— 1820.

Before me, ———————

LIST OR MANIFEST of all the Passengers taken on board the _Ship Manhattan_ whereof _Dexter Parr Jr._ — is Master, from _Liverpool_ — Burthen _Two hundred sixty Tons._ — Tons.

Dexter Parr

NAMES.	Age. Years.	Age. Months.	Sex.	Occupation.	The Country to which they severally belong.	The Country in which they intend to become inhabitants.	Died on the Voyage.
George Dickinson	41	—	man	Clerk	Great Britain	United States	
John Dickinson	37	—	female	do	—	—	
J H Hart	23	—	man	Butcher	—	—	
Tom Hart	20	—	female	do	—	—	
Julia Dunn	32	—	man	Labourer	—	—	
Dorothy Dunn	29	—	female	do	—	—	
Tom Dunn	11	—			—	—	
Billy Dunn	—	—			—	—	
— Nothingham	36	—	man	Merchant	—	—	
Eliza Nothingham	30	—	female	do	United States		
Robert Nothingham	8	—			—		
Ann Nothingham	6	—			—		
Louisa Nothingham	4	—			—		
Eliza Nothingham	1	—			—		
Robert Nothingham	28	—	man	Labourer	Great Britain		
John W Allen	37	—	man	Mechanic	—		
John Johnson	21	—	man	Draggist	—		

DISTRICT OF NEW-YORK.—PORT OF NEW YORK.

I <David Tan Jr> do solemnly, sincerely and truly <swear> that the following List or Manifest of Passengers, subscribed with my name, and now delivered by me to the Collector of the Customs for the District of New-York, contains to the best of my knowledge and belief a just and true account of all the Passengers received on board the <Ship Manhattan> whereof I am Master, from <Liverpool>

So help me God.
<David Tan Jr>

Sworn to, the <8 Augt> 182<0>
Before me, <D. Galston Clk>

LIST OR MANIFEST of all the Passengers taken on board the <Ship Manhattan> whereof <David Tan Jr> is Master, from <Liverpool> Burthen <Three hundred & ninety 79/95> Tons.

NAMES.	Age. Years.	Months.	Sex.	Occupation.	The Country to which they severally belong.	The Country in which they intend to become inhabitants.	Died on the Voyage.
George Dickinson	41–		Male	Clerk	Great Britain	United States	
Alice Dickinson	37–		Female	None			
Seth Slack	23–		Male	Butcher			
Jane Slack	20–		Female	None			
Felix Quin	32–		Male	Labourer			
Dorothy Quin	23–		Female	None			
Jane Quin	11–						
Betty Quin	7–						
Wm Nothingham	36–		Male	Merchant			
Eliza Nothingham	30–		Female	None			
Rebecca Nothingham	9–						
Ann Nothingham	8–				United States		
Levina Nothingham	6–						
Eliza Nothingham	4–						
Sarah Nothingham	1–						
John AcAteer	28–		Male	Labourer	Great Britain		
Wm Terse	37–			Merchant			
John Johnson	21–			Druggist			

PASSENGER MANIFEST OF THE SHIP MANHATTAN, 1820 (MANUSCRIPT DIVISION, THE NEW YORK PUBLIC LIBRARY)

NEW JERSEY

1664

Berthold Fernow, "West Jersey Settlers," *The New York Genealogical and Biographical Record* xxx (1899) 114–118, 175–176   **108**

    A list of people who, remaining in England, bought land there from the West Jersey Society, John Fenwick, or William Penn, or who came over and settled on the land bought by themselves or their families in England or acquired as immigrants under the law of the day.

    Names listed alphabetically, with city or county of origin, and with occupation. No ship mentioned.

1664–1703

William Nelson, ed, *Calendar of Records in the Office of the Secretary of State, 1664–1703* (Patterson, N J, The Printing Press and Publishing Co 1899) 770 p   **109**

    First series vol xxi of the *Archives of the State of New Jersey*; vol xxi of *Documents Relating to the Colonial History of the State of New Jersey.*

    Contains a number of lists of persons brought into the Province and of imported indentured servants and records of headlands for imported indentured servants and others, as well as the passenger lists of the *Thomas and Benjamin* (1684) and the *Griffin* (1689).

1675

[Passengers on the Griffin, 1675] (*In* Joseph S. Sickler *The History of Salem County New Jersey, Being the Story of John Fenwick's Colony, the Oldest English Speaking Settlement on the Delaware River*, Salem, N J, Sunbeam Publishing Co 1937, p 25)   **110**

    The passenger list of the *Griffin* (or *Griffith*) which cast anchor in the Salem River on Nov 23 1675, bringing Major John Fenwick and the first permanent English-speaking settlers in the Delaware Valley.

    A more correct and more complete list than that which appears in no 111.

    Also printed in part in no 109; in no **110A** Robert G. Johnson, "Memoir of John Fenwicke, Chief Proprietor of Salem Tenth, New Jersey," *Proceedings of the New Jersey Historical Society* iv (1849–1850) 60; and in **110B** Lewis D. Cook, "Fenwick, Adams, Hedge, and Champneys, of Salem, N.J.," *The Genealogical Magazine of New Jersey* xxxv (1960) 108.

1675–1678

Samuel Smith, *The History of the Colony of Nova-Caesaria, or New-Jersey: Containing an Account of Its First Settlement, Progressive Improvements, the Original and Present Consitution, and Other Events, to the Year 1721. With Some Particulars Since, and a Short View of Its Present State* (Burlington, N J, J. Parker 1765) 574 p   **111**

    Chapters 5 and 6, p 77–111, contain names of passengers on the *Griffith, Kent, Willing Mind, Martha, Shield* and other unspecified ships.

New Jersey, 1675–1678, continued

2d ed, published by William S. Sharp, Trenton, 1877, is identical in contents and pagination.

Also printed, omitting the *Griffith*, in   *111A* William E. Schermerhorn, *The History of Burlington, New Jersey* (Burlington 1927) p 379–380.

For a list of corrections see Robert G. Johnson, "Memoir of John Fenwicke, Chief Proprietor of Salem Tenth, New Jersey," *Proceedings of the New Jersey Historical Society* iv (1849–1850) 60.

See note for no 110.

1677–1710

Albert F. Koehler, "The Huguenots or Early French in New Jersey" (Bloomfield, N J, The Author 1955) 34 f   *112*

Mimeographed.

A history of the Huguenots who settled in New Jersey before 1710, giving time and place of birth, ancestry, time and place of arrival, marriage and death, etc, for each.

Contains an index of names.

1683–1684

See no 12.

1685

S. Helen Fields, "Convenanters and the Work of Rev. John Cuthbertson," *National Genealogical Society Quarterly* xxi (1933) 16–18   *113*

Concludes on p 17–18 with "Names of Those Who Sailed on the 'Henry and Francis,' 1685," being a list of Scotch Covenantors who landed at Perth Amboy in Dec 1685.

Published originally in   *113A* William Melancthon Glasgow, *History of the Reformed Presbyterian Church in America* (Baltimore, Hill & Harvey 1888) p 230–231; also printed in   *113B* Charlotte C. Brown and Margaret B. Lindsay, *The New Jersey Browns* (Milwaukee 1931) p 5–6; and in   *113C* William A. Whitehead, *Contributions to the Early History of Perth Amboy and Adjoining Country, with Sketches of Men and Events in New Jersey during the Provincial Era* (New York D. Appleton & Co 1856) p 28–29.

[Lists of Scotch prisoners deported to New Jersey, 1685] (*In* Robert Wodrow *The History of the Sufferings of the Church of Scotland, from the Restauration to the Revolution: Collected from the Publick Records, Original Papers, and Manuscripts of that Time, and Other Well Attested Narratives*, Edinburgh, James Watson 1722, ii 481–487)   *114*

Names of Scotch prisoners ordered deported to plantations in East New Jersey.

Also appears in iv 216–223 of the 1830 ed (Glasgow, Blackie, Fullarton & Co).

1702–1776

John R. Stevenson, "Persons Naturalized in New Jersey between 1702 and 1776," *The New York Genealogical and Biographical Record* xxviii (1897) 86–89   *115*

Collected from Allinson's *Acts of the General Assembly of the Province of New Jersey from the Surrender of the Government to Queen Anne on the 17th day of April in the Year of Our Lord 1702, to the 14th Day of January 1776* (Burlington, N J 1776).

An alphabetical list of aliens naturalized by the Assembly of New Jersey between the union of the provinces of East and West Jersey in 1702 and the commencement of the Revolutionary War. Contains name and date only, though infrequently country or origin is given.

PENNSYLVANIA

1671–1700

"Einwanderer in Pennsylvania vor 1700," *Jahrbuch für Auslanddeutsche Sippenkunde* ɪ (1936) 53–54   **116**

Appended to an article on p 44–53 by Otto Lohr entitled "Amerikadeutsche Familien des 17. Jahrhunderts."

Gives names of German families in Pennsylvania during the period covered, with place of origin frequently indicated.

No ship mentioned.

1677–1685

"A Registry of All the People in the County of Bucks within the Province of Pennsylvania That Have Come to Settle the Said County" (*In* J. H. Battle *History of Bucks County, Pennsylvania,* Philadelphia, A. Warner & Co 1887, p 672–680)   **117**

A transcription of the "Book of Arrivals" in the Register's Office, Dolyestown, Pa.

Gives name of head of household and that of his wife, the ship on which they arrived and the date of arrival, the names of their children and servants, the time of service, and wages and land allotted to them.

Also printed in **117A** "A Partial List of the Families Who Resided in Bucks County, Pennsylvania, Prior to 1687, with the Date of Their Arrival," *The Pennsylvania Magazine of History and Biography* ɪx (1885) 223–233.

1682

"The Sailing of the Ship 'Submission' in the Year 1682, with a True Copy of the Vessel's Log," *Publications of the Genealogical Society of Pennsylvania* ɪ (1895–1898) 7–13   **118**

Contains the names and ages of 49 passengers who sailed from Liverpool July 5 1682 and arrived at Choptank, Maryland, Sept 2.

"List of the Pilgrims of the 'Welcome'," *Memoirs of the Historical Society of Pennsylvania* ɪ (1864) 467–471   **119**

Republished with additions from **119A** Edward Armstrong, *An Address, Delivered at Chester before the Historical Society of Pennsylvania on the 8th of November, 1851* (Philadelphia, J. Penington 1852) p 22–25; also printed in **119B** E. B. Cogwill, "The Passengers on the 'Welcome'," *Transactions of the Kansas State Historical Society* vɪ (1900) 56–59.

The list is not included in the 1826 ed of the *Memoirs*. Material gathered from many sources; the list contains 99 of the estimated 100 passengers who accompanied William Penn.

Marion Balderston, "The Real *Welcome* Passengers," *The Huntington Library Quarterly* xxvɪ (1962) 31–56   **120**

A critical examination of the passenger list of the *Welcome* given in no 119, proving only 43 of the 99 passengers listed there as having arrived for certain on the ship and giving the names of 17 probable passengers.

Pennsylvania, 1682, continued

George E. McCracken, "Welcome Notes," *The American Genealogist* xxxviii (1962) 152–163; xxxix (1963) 4–7, 164–169   **121**

New information concerning some of the passengers on the *Welcome*. Scrutinizes a dozen hypothetical lists of passengers on the *Welcome*, no two of them alike.
To be continued.

1682–1683

[Passengers on the *Friends' Adventure*, 1682, and the *Endeavor*, 1683] (*In* J. H. Battle *History of Bucks County, Pennsylvania*, Philadelphia, A. Warner & Co 1887, p 440–441)   **122**

Contains the names of several passengers arriving on the *Friends' Adventure*, July 1682, and on the *Endeavor*, July 1683.

1682–1684

Charles H. Browning, *Welsh Settlement of Pennsylvania* (Philadelphia, William J. Campbell 1912) 631 p   **123**

A history of the settlement of "Welsh tract" lands granted by William Penn, 1681, containing the names of a great many early emigrants and the ships on which some of them arrived.

1682–1687

"A Partial List of the Families Who Arrived at Philadelphia between 1682 and 1687. With the Dates of Their Arrival," *The Pennsylvania Magazine of History and Biography* viii (1884) 328–340   **124**

From the original in the possession of the Historical Society of Pennsylvania.
A list of persons, mostly servants, arriving at Philadelphia during the period covered. Name of ship in which they arrived often indicated.
Also printed in **124A** J. Smith Futhey and Gilbert Cope, *History of Chester County, Pennsylvania, with Genealogical and Biographical Sketches* (Philadelphia, Louis H. Everts 1881) p 22–24.

1682–1750

Albert Cook Myers, *Quaker Arrivals at Philadelphia, 1682–1750; Being a List of Certificates of Removal Received at Philadelphia Monthly Meeting of Friends* (Philadelphia, Ferris & Leach 1902) 131 p   **125**

"Second edition"; published originally by Ferris & Leach, Philadelphia, 1902. 2d ed reissued in facsimile by the Genealogical Publishing Co, Baltimore, 1957.
A chronological listing of Quaker immigrants registered upon their arrival in Philadelphia according to their certificates of removal from their respective meetings of Friends to which they belonged in other countries.
Contains an index of surnames.
No ship mentioned.

"List of Certificates of Removal from Ireland Received at the Monthly Meetings of Friends in Pennsylvania, 1682–1750; with Genealogical Notes from Friends' Records of Ireland and Pennsylvania, Genealogies, County Histories, and Other Books and Manuscripts" (*In* Albert Cook Myers *Immigration of the Irish Quakers into Pennsylvania, 1682–1750*, Swarthmore, The Author 1902, p 277–390)   **126**

Nature of contents and arrangement as in no 125.

Names on these certificates contained within the index to the volume.

No ship mentioned.

1683–1684

See no 12.

1683–1709

William I. Hull, *William Penn and the Dutch Quaker Migration to Pennsylvania* (Swarthmore, Pa, Swarthmore College 1935) 445 p   **127**

Swarthmore College Monographs on Quaker History Number Two.

Contains a list of "The Dutch Pioneers of Germantown," 1683, p 395–398, and "Dutch and German Settlers in Germantown, 1683–1709," p 399–421.

Gives a complete list of early Dutch and German settlers in Germantown with place of origin designated. Both Dutch and German forms of the name are provided.

No ship mentioned.

Supplementary to no 125.

1683–1777

"General List of Huguenot Immigrants to Pennsylvania" (*In* Ammon Stapleton *Memorials of the Huguenots in America, with Special Reference to Their Emigration to Pennsylvania*, Carlisle, Pa, Huguenot Publishing Co 1901, p 147–157)   **128**

An alphabetical list of immigrants to Pennsylvania during the Provincial period who are believed to have been of Huguenot origin. In large part these names are extracts from the more complete lists in nos 144 and 145.

No ship mentioned.

1684–1685

See no 199.

1691–1692

"Naturalizations, Germantown, Pa. 3/7/1691/92; Copia Naturalisationis of Francis Daniel Pastorius and of 61 Persons More of German Town from Willam Penn, Esq.," *National Genealogical Society Quarterly* xxviii (1940) 7–8   **129**

From a record of the Rolls Office, Philadelphia, now in the Juniata College Library, Huntington, Pa.

A proclamation of William Penn declaring Francis Daniel Pastorius and 61 other foreigners freemen of the Province of Pennsylvania. Two additional names have been added by a later owner of the document.

Pennsylvania, continued

1697–1698

W. F. Corbit, "Welsh Emigration to Pennsylvania. An Old Charter Party," *The Pennsylvania Magazine of History and Biography* I (1877) 330–332
130

Articles of freightment, made Mar 7 1697/8 between Owen Thomas, owner of the ship *William Galley*, and David Powell, John Morris, and 17 others, for passage to Pennsylvania.

1697–1707

See no 14.

1697–1815

See no 15.

1706–1795

Albert Bernhardt Faust, *Lists of Swiss Emigrants in the Eighteenth Century to the American Colonies* (Washington, D C, The National Genealogical Society 1920–1925) 2 v
131

Vol I contains lists of Swiss emigrants from the Canton of Zurich to Carolina and Pennsylvania, 1734–1744, arranged chronologically by districts and villages; vol II contains lists of such emigrants from the Cantons of Bern and Basil, 1709–1795. Names of emigrants from Bern listed alphabetically; those from Basil are arranged chronologically, then by districts and villages.

Vol II compiled by Albert Bernhardt Faust and Gaius Marcus Brumbaugh.

Each volume has an index to surnames.

Supplementary to no 146.

1709

See no 16.

1709–1768

Friedrich Krebs, *Emigrants from the Palatinate to the American Colonies in the 18th Century. Edited, with an Introduction, by Milton Rubincam* (Norristown, Pennsylvania German Society 1953) 32 p
132

Pennsylvania German Society Special Study Number One.

From church records of Freckenfeld, Billigheim, Thaleischweiler, Essenheim, Niederkirchen, Obermoschel, and Moersfeld in the Bayerisches Staatsarchiv at Speyer.

An alphabetical list of emigrants and families, giving place of origin and arrival, ship name, when identified, and date of exit and/or arrival.

1709–1785

Adolf Gerber, *Beiträge zur Auswanderung nach Amerika im 18. Jahrhundert aus Altwürttembergischen Kirchenbüchern* (Stuttgart, J. F. Steinkopf [1928]) 32 p
133

List of emigrants from the duchy of Württemberg arranged alphabetically under the town from which they came. Made up from local church records.

No ship mentioned in this or the supplementary vol (no 134). However, ship names, extracted from nos 145 and 146 and from other sources, have been included in the English ed (no 135).

—— *Neue Beiträge zur Auswanderung nach Amerika im 18. Jahrhundert aus Altwürttembergischen Kirchenbuchern unter Hinzuziehung anderer Quellen* (Stuttgart, J. F. Steinkopf [1929?]) 44 p **134**

A supplementary vol compiled from broader source material, including state archives. Arrangement as before, but supplement contains an index of surnames which is lacking from the original list.

—— "Emigrants from Wuerttemberg; the Adolf Gerber Lists. Edited by Donald Herbert Yoder, Union Theological Seminary," *The Pennsylvania German Folklore Society Yearbook* x (1945) 103–237 **135**

An English ed of the original and supplementary Gerber lists combined. Names listed alphabetically, with reference to Gerber volume. Where possible, ship names supplied from nos 145 and 146 and from other sources. See note for no 176.

1709–1786

Otto Langguth, "Pennsylvania German Pioneers from the County of Wertheim. Translated and Edited by Don Yoder, Ph.D., Muhlenberg College," *The Pennsylvania German Folklore Society Yearbook* xii (1947) 147–289 **136**

Compiled from ms materials in the Princely Archive of Löwenstein-Wertheim-Rosenberg.

Alphabetical list of 272 emigrants from Wertheim in Franconia, with ship identifications supplied from no 146.

Also printed in **136A** Otto Langguth, "Auswanderer aus der Grafschaft Wertheim," *Familiengeschichtliche Blätter* xxx (1932) 53–60, 109–124, 155–164, 205–208, 263–270, 299–304, 343–352 and reprinted in the *Jahrbuch des Historischen Vereins Alt-Wertheim* for 1935.

1709–1798

Adolf Gerber, *Die Nassau-Dillenburger Auswanderung nach Amerika im 18 Jahrhundert; das Verhalten der Regierungen dazu und die Späteren Shicksale der Auswanderer* (Flensburg, Flensburger Nachrichten, Deutscher Verlag G. m. b. H. 1930) 51 p **137**

Made up mostly from ms sources in the Staatsarchiv, Wiesbaden.

Divided into three periods, with emigrants listed in each alphabetically under the town from which they came.

Contains an index of surnames.

No ship mentioned.

See no 16.

1718–1742

Pennsylvania (Colony). Provincial Council, *Minutes of the Provincial Council of Pennsylvania, from the Organization to the Termination of the*

Pennsylvania, 1718–1742, continued

Proprietary Government. Published by the State (Harrisburg, T. Fenn &
Co, III, 1840, 299–301, 303–305, 307, 346–348, 350–351, 390–392, 409–411,
414, 436–437, 440–442, 444, 457, 460–461, 483–490, 498–501, 554–559, 564,
614–616, 642–643, 647; IV, 1851, 58–60, 72–73, 99–100, 331–332)   *138*

Volumes III–IV of the *Colonial Records of Pennsylvania.*
Lists of Palatines arriving in Pennsylvania between 1718 and 1742.
First 3 volumes of the *Colonial Records* issued by Theophilus Fenn, Harrisburg,
1838–1840; volumes IV–XVI issued by T. Fenn & Co, Harrisburg, 1851–1853; volumes I–III reprinted by J. Severns & Co, Philadelphia, 1852. Paging of reprint volume III not identical with that of the 1st ed; consequently, volume III of the reprint
ed has been designated *138A* for inclusion in the analytical index of ship names.
Also printed in part in no 144.

1720–1786

Fritz Braun and Friedrich Krebs, "Pennsylvania Dutch Pioneers from
South Palatine Parishes," *The Pennsylvania Dutchman* VIII (Spring 1957)
39–42   *139*

From Lutheran Church Registers of the villages of Freimersheim, Freisbach, Gom-
mersheim, Minfeld and Weingarten; Reformed Church Registers of Zeiskam and Ober-
lustadt; the *Ausfautheiakten Germersheim*; the Electoral Palatine Archives for
Westheim; the Archives of the Johannite Order in the Palatine State Archives in Speyer;
and from materials in the *Heimatstelle Pfalz* in Kaiserslautern.
Emigrants grouped under villages whence they originated. In many cases ship names
and arrival dates have been supplied from no 146.
Published originally in *139A* Fritz Braun and Friedrich Krebs, "Amerikaauswan-
derer aus dem 18. Jahrhunderts aus Südpfälzischen Gemeinden," *Mitteilungen zur Wanderungsgeschichte der Pfälzer* (*Beilage zu Pfälzische Familien- und Wappenkunde*) folge
5 (1956) 29–36; folge 6 (1956) 37–44; folge 11–12 (1957) 83–84, and reprinted
from there in *139B* heft 2 of *Schriften zur Wanderungsgeschichte der Pfälzer* (Ludwigshafen am Rhein, Richard Louis Verlag 1956) 20 p.

1726–1727

Friedrich Krebs, "Zur Frühauswanderung aus dem Kurpfälzischen Oberamt Heidelberg nach Amerika (1726–27)," *Südwestdeutsche Blätter für
Familien- und Wappenkunde* X (1958) 512   *140*

From protocols in the Generallandesarchiv, Karlsruhe.
A record of the early emigration from Heidelberg to America.
Also printed in no 141.
See also nos 156 and 162
No ship mentioned.

1726–1777

Friedrich Krebs, "Annotations to Strassburger and Hinke's Pennsylvania
German Pioneers," *The Pennsylvania Genealogical Magazine* XXI (1960)
235–248   *141*

From records in the State Archives at Karlsruhe, the State Archives at Ludwigsburg,
the City Archives at Oppenheim, and the State Archives at Speyer.

Contains names of emigrants from Heidelberg, Württemberg, Oppenheim, and from the present-day Pfalz and the regions of Nahe and Hunsrück.
Gives name of ship and arrival date when known.
A composite of nos 140, 152, 156, 162, 163, 167 and 170.

1727

Frank Reid Differderffer, "The German Immigration into Pennsylvania through the Port of Philadelphia, and 'The Redemptioners'," *The Pennsylvania-German Society Proceedings and Addresses* x (1900) 328 p *142*

P 40–42 contains "A List of Ye Palatine Passengers Imported in Ye Ship William and Sarah, Will'm Hill, Mast'r, from Rotterdam, Phlid'a Ye 18 Sept'bre 1727." P 213–216 contains a partial list of passengers who arrived on the *Britannia*, Sept 18 1773.
The list of the *William and Sarah* also printed in nos 145 and 146.
See no 186.

1727–1740

Charles R. Roberts, "Germanic Immigrants Named in Early Pennsylvania Ship Lists," *The Pennsylvania German Society Proceedings and Addresses* xxxix (1928) 20 p *143*

A general discussion of the passenger lists preserved in the State Library (Department of Public Records) in Harrisburg. Excerpts names from various lists and gives biographical data on some of the immigrants.

1727–1776

Daniel Israel Rupp, *A Collection of Upwards of Thirty Thousand Names of German, Swiss, Dutch, French and Other Immigrants in Pennsylvania from 1727 to 1776, with a Statement of the Names of Ships, Whence They Sailed, and the Date of their Arrival at Philadelphia, Chronologically Arranged, Together with the Necessary Historical and Other Notes, also, an Appendix Containing Lists of More Than One Thousand German and French Names in New York Prior to 1712* (Leipzig, Degener & Co 1931) 478, 89 p *144*

Third ed. Begun originally in monthly parts, but 1st ed issued from stereotyped plates at Harrisburg 1856; 2d ed Philadelphia 1876. 3d ed contains corresponding text in German and has added t-p *Chronologisch Geordnete Sammlung von Mehr als 30,000 Namen.* . . .
Namenregister zu J. Daniel Rupp's "Chronologisch Geordneter Sammlung von Mehr als 30,000 Namen . . ." Angefertigt nach der Ausgabe von 1880 durch Ernst Wecken (Leipzig, Degener & Co 1931) 89 p at end. The 1931 ed alone contains this index of names.
Another index by Marvin V. Koger, *Index to the Names of 30,000 Immigrants, German, Swiss, Dutch and French into Pennsylvania, 1727–1776, Supplementing the l. Daniel Rupp, Ship Load Volume,* issued by the compiler (Pennington Gap, Va 1935, 232 p) in mimeographed form.
P 449 contains "Names of the First Palatines in North Carolina, as Early as 1709 and 1710"; p 449–451 contain "Names of Males, Salzburgers, Settled in Georgia, 1734 to 1741."
See note for no 146.

Pennsylvania, continued

1727–1808

William Henry Egle, ed, *Names of Foreigners Who Took the Oath of Allegiance to the Province and State of Pennsylvania, 1727–1775, with the Foreign Arrivals, 1786–1808* (Harrisburg, E. K. Meyers 1892) 787 p   **145**

Ser 2 vol xvii of the *Pennsylvania Archives*.
Very comprehensive. Taken from the original mss among the State Archives.
Contains an index of surnames.
See note for no 146.

Ralph Beaver Strassburger, *Pennsylvania German Pioneers; a Publication of the Original Lists of Arrivals in the Port of Philadelphia from 1727 to 1808. Edited by William John Hinke* (Norristown, Pennsylvania German Society 1934) 3 vols   **146**

Volumes xlii–xliv of the *Pennsylvania German Society Proceedings*.
A revision and addition to the mateial contained in nos 144 and 145 prepared and edited with great accuracy. For comparative criticism see review by Albert B. Faust in the *Pennsylvania Magazine of History and Biography* lix (1935) 432–436.
Contains 29,887 names from (A) captains' lists; (B) lists of signers of the oath of allegiance; (C) lists of signers of the oath of abjuration. Volume i contains captains' lists from 1727 to 1775; volume ii contains facsimiles of all signatures in lists B and C; volume iii contains captains' lists from 1785–1808 and indices to captains, ships, ports of departure and surnames in all volumes. Volume ii not analyzed in "Index of Ship Names" below.

1728–1749

William John Hinke and John Baer Stoudt, eds, "A List of German Immigrants to the American Colonies from Zweibruecken in the Palatinate, 1728–1749," *The Pennsylvania German Folklore Society Yearbook* i (1936) 101–124   **147**

Extracted from a document in the Bavarian State Archives at Speyer, Germany. The German text of this document was published by Bryant Wiest of Elizabethville, Pa, in *Valley Citizen*, a weekly newspaper of Valley View, Pa, in 1933.
A list of 404 emigrants destined for Pennsylvania and Carolina. Names grouped chronologically under the governmental districts from which they came.
See note for no 175.

1730

Fritz Braun, *Auswanderer aus der Umgebung von Ludwigshafen a. Rh. auf dem Schiff "Thistle of Glasgow" 1730* (Neustadt an der Aisch, Buchdruckerei Ph. C. W. Schmidt 1959) 21 p   **148**

Folge 8 of *Schriften zur Wanderungsgeschichte der Pfälzer*.
Reprinted from **148A** *Mitteilungen zur Wanderungsgeschichte der Pfälzer* (*Beilage zu Pfälzische Familien- und Wappenkunde*) folge 3–4 (1959) 253–272.
Contains the names of 77 families or individuals from the Ludwigshafen area who were among the 260 Palatines on board the *Thistle* which landed at Philadelphia on

August 29 1730. Where possible, traces their earlier and later histories from ms and printed sources both in Germany and in America.

The list of names without genealogical data originally appeared in *148B* Fritz Braun, "Auswanderer aus der Umgebung von Ludwigshafen am Rhein auf dem Schiff 'Thistle of Glasgow' 1730," *Mitteilungen zur Wanderungsgeschichte der Pfälzer* folge 5 (1953) 31–32. The names of 13 persons whose home villages were positively identified appeared in *148C* "Fritz Braun, "Palatines on the Ship 'Thistle of Glasgow' (1730)," *The Pennsylvania Dutchman* v (March 1 1954) 13.

1732–1733

"Passengers from the Rhineland to Pennsylvania," *Publications of The Genealogical Society of Pennsylvania* xiv (1942) 79   **149**

Fifteen Palatines advised by an advertisement in the *Pennsylvania Gazette* of Mar 22 1732–3 to make speedy payment or give security for their passages or to expect prosecution.

No ship mentioned.

1732–1773

Friedrich Krebs, "Einige Amerika-Auswanderer des 18. Jahrhunderts," *Senftenegger Monatsblatt für Genealogie und Heraldik* v (1960–1963) 79–82   **150**

From documents in the Stadtarchiv, Wachenheim, and the Gemeindearchiv, Hassloch.

Lists of emigrants from Wachenheim and Hassloch to Pennsylvania or Carolina, 1732–1773.

No ship mentioned.

1732–1785

Friedrich Krebs, "Pennsylvania Dutch Pioneers," *The Pennsylvania Dutchman* vi (June 1954) 40, (September 1954) 37, (Winter 1954–1955) 39, (Spring 1955) 37–38; vii (Winter 1956) 38–39, (Spring 1956) 38–39; viii (Summer 1956) 57–59   **151**

From source materials in state and municipal archives and from church records of various towns of the Palatine.

Gives names and some genealogical data on several thousand emigrants from Germany to Pennsylvania with arrival dates and ship names supplied from no 146.

Translated by Don Yoder.

1733–1777

Friedrich Krebs, "Amerika-Auswanderer des 18. Jahrhunderts aus der Heutigen Pfalz und der Nahe- und Hunsrückgegend," *Mitteilungen zur Wanderungsgeschichte der Pfälzer (Beilage zu Pfälzische Familien- und Wappenkunde)* folge 11–12 (1954) 62–66   **152**

From records filed in the Staatsarchiv, Speyer.

Supplies ship name and arrival date when known.

Also printed in no 141.

Pennsylvania, continued

1734–1735

"Early Swiss Settlers," *Notes and Queries Historical, Biographical and Genealogical Relating Chiefly to Interior Pennsylvania. Annual Volume, 1900* (1901) 121–122   **153**

From a pamphlet entitled Der *Hinkinde Bott von Carolina* (*The Limping Messanger from Carolina, or the Description of a Journey from Zurich to Rotterdam, by Ludwig Weber, from Wallisellen,* Zurich 1735), found by William J. Hinke, the contributor of the list, among Swiss archives.

Contains the names of 48 Swiss emigrants who left Zurich in Oct 1734 and arrived in Philadelphia on May 29 1735 on the ship *Mercury.*

A more complete list of this voyage, giving 186 names including children under 16, may be found in nos 144 and 145.

1734–1752

Ernst Steinemann, ed, "A List of Eighteenth-Century Emigrants from the Canton of Schaffhausen to the American Colonies, 1734–1752. With an Introduction by Dr. Don Yoder," *The Pennsylvania German Folklore Society Yearbook* xvi (1951) 185–196   **154**

An alphabetical listing of 122 heads of families or individuals destined for Pennsylvania, Halifax, Nova Scotia, and Carolina.

Only a few ships mentioned.

Also printed in **154A** Ernst Steinemann, "Zur Schaffhauserischen Auswanderung," *Beiträge zur Vaterländischen Geschichte Herausgegeben vom Historisch-antiquarischen Verein des Kantons Schaffhausen* xiii (1936).

1734–1765

John W. Jordan, "Moravian Immigration to Pennsylvania, 1734–1765," *The Pennsylvania Magazine of History and Biography* xxxiii (1909) 228–248   **155**

A collection of several ships lists in chronological order with descriptive commentary. The compiler has also prepared a list of the immigrants from 1765 to 1800. The manuscript, as yet unpublished, is in the Manuscript Department of the Historical Society of Pennsylvania.

See no 164.

1737–1754

Friedrich Krebs, "Die Amerikaauswanderung aus dem Kurpfälzischen Oberamt Heidelberg in den Jahren 1737, 1738, 1751, 1753 und 1754," *Badische Heimat* xxxviii (1958) 303–304   **156**

From protocols in the Generallandesarchiv, Karlsruhe.
Also printed in no 141.
Supplementary to nos 140 and 162.
No ship mentioned.

1738

Harrold E. Gillingham, "Philadelphia Arrivals, 1738," *Publications of The Genealogical Society of Pennsylvania* xii (1934) 150　　　**157**

List of 7 indentured servants on the *Elizabeth* from London, July 1738. From an ms invoice in the Historical Society of Pennsylvania.

1738–1750

Hugo Froehlich, "Pioneers from Staudernheim," *The Pennsylvania Dutchman* viii (Fall-Winter 1956–1957) 43–46　　　**158**

From the Lutheran Church Register of the village of Staudernheim.

Includes the names of 90 emigrants to Pennsylvania, mostly in the years 1739 and 1741, arranged alphabetically by family, with arrival dates and ship identifications supplied in some cases from no 146.

Published originally in　**158A** Hugo Fröhlich, "Auswanderer im Lutherischen Kirchenbuch von Staudernheim an der Nahe," *Mitteilungen zur Wanderungsgeschichte der Pfälzer (Beilage zu Pfälzische Familien- und Wappenkunde)* folge 10 (1954) 55–62.

Translation here by Don Yoder.

See no 17-1.

1738–1765

Freidrich Krebs, "Auswanderer nach den Nordamerikanischen Kolonien in Lutherischen Kirchenbuch von Thaleischweiler," *Mitteilungen zur Wanderungsgeschichte der Pfälzer (Beilage zu Pfälzische Familien- und Wappenkunde)* folge 3–4 (1952) 21–24　　　**159**

An alphabetical list of emigrants to Pennsylvania, as indicated by entries in the Lutheran parish register at Thaleischweiler.

When possible, ship name and arrival date have been supplied from no 146.

1740–1743

Louis F. Middlebrook, "The Ship *Mary* of Philadelphia, 1740," *The Pennsylvania Magazine of History and Biography* lviii (1934) 127–151　　**160**

A general account of the building and early history of the *Mary*. P 150 contains a list of passengers on a trip to Philadelphia in 1743.

1740–1773

"Persons Naturalized in the Province of Pennsylvania," *Pennsylvania Archives* 2d ser ii (1876) 293–415　　　**161**

Lists of foreign Protestants naturalized in Pennsylvania during the period covered. Gives name, place of residence, and date of taking of the sacrament.

Slightly more complete and more time-inclusive than the list in no 19.

Pennsylvania, continued

1741-1748

Friedrich Krebs, "Zur Amerikaauswanderung aus dem Kurpfälzischen Oberamt Heidelberg 1741–1748," *Zeitschrift für die Geschichte des Oberrheins* cvi (neue folge lxvii) (1958) 485–486   **162**

From protocols in the Generallandesarchiv, Karlsruhe.
Also printed in no 141.
Supplementary to nos 140 and 156.
No ship mentioned.

1742-1749

Friedrich Krebs, "Amerika-Auswanderer aus dem Oberamt Oppenheim 1742–49," *Hessische Familienkunde* iii (1954–1956) 342–343   **163**

From protocols in the Stadtarchiv, Oppenheim.
Names of persons permitted to emigrate to Pennsylvania, with ship name and arrival date supplied when known.
Also printed in no 141.

1742-1799

John W. Jordan, "A Register of Members of the Moravian Church Who Emigrated to Pennsylvania, 1742–1767," *Notes and Queries: Historical, Biographical and Genealogical: Relating Chiefly to Interior Pennsylvania* 4th ser i (1893) 162–163, 167–168, 169–170, 174–175, 208–૮ ٔ1, 303–304; ii (1895) 1–3   **164**

Lists of Moravian arrivals at Philadelphia and New York, whence the majority migrated to Bethlehem and a few to North Carolina.
Supplementary to no 155.

1745-1746

George W. Neible, "Servants and Apprentices Bound and Assigned before James Hamilton Mayor of Philadelphia, 1745," *The Pennsylvania Magazine of History and Biography* xxx (1906) 348–352, 427–436; xxxi (1907) 83–102, 195–206, 351–367, 461–473; xxxii (1908) 88–103, 237–249, 351–370   **165**

A chronological list of immigrant servants indentured in Philadelphia between Oct 2 1745 and Oct 7 1746.

1746-1747

"List of Servants Who Sailed from Dublin February 25th 1746/7 on the Euryal, and Arrived at Philadelphia April 11th.," *The Pennsylvania Magazine of History and Biography* xxvi (1902) 287   **166**

List of servants, all women.

1748–1768

Friedrich Krebs, "Einige Amerika-Auswanderer des 18. Jahrhunderts," *Senftenegger Monatsblatt für Genealogie und Heraldik* IV (1956–1959) 195–198   **167**

Advertisements for missing heirs from the *Kayserliche Reichs-Oberpostamts-Zeitung* (Frankfurt a. M.) 1776–1788.
Arrival dates supplied from no 146 when known.
Also printed in no 141.
No ship mentioned.

1749

Friedrich Krebs, "Einige Amerika-Auswanderer des 18. Jahrhunderts," *Senftenegger Monatsblatt für Genealogie und Heraldik* V (1960–1963) 123–126   **168**

From protocols in the Generallandesarchiv, Karlsruhe.
A list of emigrants from Baden-Durlach to Pennsylvania, 1749.
See nos 171, 177 and 181.
Also printed in no 141.
No ship mentioned.

1749–1750

Friedrich Krebs, "Pennsylvania Pioneers from the Neckar Valley, 1749–1750," *The Pennsylvania Dutchman* V (June 1953) 13   **169**

From Protocols of the Districts of Heidelberg and Mosbach, now part of the state of Württemberg-Baden.
Arranged chronologically under districts, with ship and arrival date often supplied from no 146.
Previously published in German in *Badische Heimat* (Freiburg), May 1953.

1749–1751

Friedrich Krebs, "Einige Amerika-Auswanderer des 18. Jahrhunderts aus Württemberg," *Südwestdeutsche Blätter für Familien- und Wappenkunde* IX (1957) 442–443   **170**

From protocols in the Staatsfilialarchiv, Ludwigsburg.
Six emigrants from Württemberg, with identifications as to ship and/or arrival date.
Also printed in no 141.

1749–1755

Friedrich Krebs, "Emigrants from Baden-Durlach to Pennsylvania, 1749–1755," *National Genealogical Society Quarterly* XLV (1957) 30–31   **171**

From original records of the Court Council and Revenue Office of Baden-Durlach.
List of 36 emigrants to Pennsylvania, 1749–1755, but mostly in the year 1751, with ship name and arrival date frequently provided.
See nos 168, 177 and 181.

Pennsylvania, continued

1749–1764

Friedrich Krebs, "18th Century Emigrants from Edenkoben in the Palatinate," *The Pennsylvania Dutchman* IV (Jan 1 1953) 9   **172**

A General discussion of the emigration from Edenkoben to America during the 18th-century. Contains the names of a number of emigrants.

Previously published in German in the *Geschäfts Anzeiger* (Edenkoben) of Aug 2 1952; translation by Don Yoder.

1749–1768

Fritz Braun, "18th Century Palatine Emigrants from the Ludwigshafen Area," *The Pennsylvania Dutchman* V (Mar 1 1954) 13   **173**

From the Protocols of the District of Neustadt.

Names of 8 emigrants destined for Pennsylvania and 1 for Nova Scotia, with ship name and date of arrival often supplied.

1750

Friedrich Krebs, "Palatine Emigrants from the District of Neustadt, 1750," *The Pennsylvania Dutchman* V (May 1953) 9   **174**

Extracted from the Protocols of the District of Neustadt in the Palatine State Archives at Speyer.

Names of 13 persons applying for permission to emigrate, with ship and date of arrival supplied from no 146.

1750–1771

Friedrich Krebs, ed, "A List of German Immigrants to the American Colonies from Zweibruecken in the Palatinate, 1750–1771. With an Introduction by Dr. Don Yoder," *The Pennsylvania German Folklore Society Yearbook* XVI (1951) 171–183   **175**

From a ms in the Kirchschaffnei Archiv in Zweibrücken.

Lists 152 emigrants to Pennsylvania and Carolina, of whom 45 are identified in no 146.

Names arranged chronologically under the governmental districts from which they came.

Also printed in   **175A** Friedrich Krebs, "Eine Liste Deutscher Auswanderer nach den Amerikanischen Kolonien aus Zweibrücken in der Pfalz 1750–1771," *Familie und Volk* I (1952) 29–32.

Additional material to no 147.

1751–1754

Friedrich Krebs, "Zur Amerika-Auswanderung des 18. Jahrhunderts aus Altwürttemberg hauptsächlich aus dem ehemaligen Oberamt Urach," *Südwestdeutsche Blatter für Familien- und Wappenkunde* IX (1957) 464–465   **176**

From prctocols and acts of the government of Würtemberg in the Staatsfilialarchiv in Ludwigsburg.

A list of emigrants from Dettingen, with ship names and arrival dates supplied from no 146.

Supplementary to no 135.

1752

Friedrich Krebs, "Pennsylvania Dutch Pioneers from Baden-Durlach: 1752," *The Pennsylvania Dutchman* VIII (Summer-Fall 1957) 48   **177**

Compiled from protocols of the Council and Revenue Chamber of Baden-Durlach, preserved in the General State Archives of Baden in Karlsruhe.

Gives name, goal of emigration (destination) and protocol number only.

Supplementary to nos 168, 171 and 181.

Originally published as "Amerika-Auswanderer aus Baden-Durlach im Jahre 1752," *Senftenegger Monatsblatt für Genealogie und Heraldik* III (1955–1956) 289–292.

No ship mentioned.

———"Beiträge zur Amerikaauswanderung des 18. Jahrhunderts aus Altwürttemberg," *Südwestdeutsche Blätter für Familien- und Wappenkunde* XI (1959–1962) 186–189   **178**

Lists of persons emigrating from Freudenstadt to Pennsylvania in 1752 following an act passed by the Würtemberg goverment on May 7 of that year permitting it. A great many of these sailed on the *Duke of Wirtemberg.*

From a copy of the act in the Staatsfilialarchiv in Ludwigsburg.

"Moravian Pioneers in the Swatara Valley, 1752," *The Pennsylvania Dutchman* II (Dec 15 1950) 6   **179**

The names of 10 Moravian emigrants belonging to the Congregation at Swatara, 1752.

Transcribed from the original document, "Catalogus der Geschwister in Swatara den 25. Oct. 1752," now in the Moravian Archives at Bethlehem, by William J. Hinke.

No ship mentioned.

"Moravian Brethren in Heidelberg, 1752," *The Pennsylvania Dutchman* II (Jan 1 1951) 6   **180**

A list of Moravian emigrants belonging to the Congregation at Heidelberg, Pennsylvania, 1752.

Transcribed from the original document, "Catalogus der Geschwister in Heidelberg, Oct. 1752," now in the Moravian Archives in Bethlehem, by William J. Hinke.

1753

Friedrich Krebs, "Amerika-Auswanderer aus Baden-Durlach im Jahre 1753," *Senftenegger Monatsblatt für Genealogie und Heraldik* IV (1956–1959) 79–80   **181**

Source and arrangement identical with no 177.

Supplementary to nos 168, 171 and 177.

Pennsylvania, continued

1754–1768

Friedrich Krebs, "More 18th Century Emigrants from the Palatinate," *The Pennsylvania Dutchman* v (Mar 1 1954) 12   **182**

From Protocols of the District of Neustadt.
10 Emigrants granted permission to go to America, with ship names and dates of departure supplied.

1758

R. G. Smith, "German Families," *The Pennsylvania Magazine of History and Biography* xxxiii (1909) 501–502   **183**

A list of German families arriving at Philadelphia from Holland. Gives name and origin only.
From an advertisement in Henry Miller's *Staats Bote* of Feb 9 1758.
No ship mentioned.

1771–1773

"Record of Indentures of Individuals Bound Out as Apprentices, Servants, Etc. and of German and Other Redemptioners in the Office of the Mayor of the City of Philadelphia, October 3, 1771, to October 5, 1773," *The Pennsylvania-German Society Proceedings and Addresses* xvi (1905–1907) 325 p   **184**

From the original volume in possession of The American Philosophical Society, Philadelphia.
Chronological list of persons indentured, giving name, port of departure, to whom indentured, residence here, occupation, and term of service.
Duplicated in part in no 185.
No ship mentioned.

1772–1773

"Record of Servants and Apprentices Bound and Assigned before Hon. John Gibson, Mayor of Philadelphia, December 5th, 1772 – May 21, 1773," *The Pennsylvania Magazine of History and Biography* xxxiii (1909) 475–491; xxxiv (1910) 99–121, 213–228   **185**

Copied from original Record Book in the Manuscript Department of the Historical Society of Pennsylvania.
See no 184.

1773

"A List of German Emigrants, 1773," *The Pennsylvania Magazine of History and Biography* xiii (1889) 113–115   **186**

From a manuscript in the Historical Society of Pennsylvania.
Gives the names of 53 German passengers who arrived on the ship *Britannia* on Sept 18 1773, together with the amount of their passage money and expenses due

Messrs Joshua Fisher & Sons, Philadelphia. Contains the names of several persons not included in the incomplete list of the voyage in nos 144, 145 and 146.
Also printed in no 142.

1774–1775

See no 21.

1775

"List of Arrivals per 'Pennsylvania Packet,' 1775," *The Pennsylvania Magazine of History and Biography* xviii (1894) 379   **187**

Copied from original ms in the collection of the Historical Society of Pennsylvania.
A list of indentured servants bound for Philadelphia March 15 1775.

1789–1880

United States. Work Projects Administration, *Index to Records of Aliens' Declarations of Intention and/or Oaths of Allegiance, 1789–1880, in United States Circuit Court, United States District Court, Supreme Court of Pennsylvania, Quarter Sessions Court, Court of Common Pleas, Philadelphia. Compiled by Work Projects Administration, Project No. 20837. Sponsored by Pennsylvania Historical Commission* (Harrisburg 1940?) 11 vols   **188**

Section ii, *Alphabetical Index of Naturalization Records, 1794–1880*, of *Maritime Records Port of Philadelphia* (Pennsylvania Historical Survey, Work Projects Administration; Sponsor, Pennsylvania Historical Commission, Harrisburg).
Reproduced from typewritten copy.
From original documents in the custody of the various courts concerned.
An alphabetical index of persons applying for naturalization before courts in Philadelphia during the period covered.
Entries include name of applicant, country of former allegiance, court of record, and date of declaration of intention and/or oath of allegiance.
No ship mentioned in this section.

1791–1792

Luther R. Kelker, "List of Foreigners Who Arrived at Philadelphia, 1791–1792," *The Pennsylvania Magazine of History and Biography* xxiv (1900) 187–194, 334–342   **189**

Supplementary to no 145 but included in part in no 146.

1796–1830

Don Yoder, ed, "Lehigh County Naturalization Records," *The Pennsylvania Dutchman* i (May 5 1959) 6; ii (Jan 1950) 6   **190**

A list of German and Swiss emigrants who petitioned for naturalization before the Court of Common Pleas of Lehigh County in accordance with a federal law of 1798.
Copied from original papers in the Prothonotary's Office of the Lehigh County Courthouse in Allentown.
Entries include name, place of origin, and date of arrival.
No ship mentioned.

Pennsylvania, continued

1803–1806

See no 25.

1804

"List of German Passengers Arrived in the Port, Philadelphia, in the Ship Margaret, from Amsterdam, C. E. Gardner, Master, September 19th, 1804. As Taken from the Original Immigrant List on File in the Division of Public Records, Harrisburg, Pa.," *Journal of the Lycoming Historical Society* I (1956) 9–12   **191**

    Contains 91 names, with size of household and age, place of birth, county and country of origin, occupation, and physical characteristics of head of household.
    Also printed in nos 145 and 146.

1811

See no 27.

1815–1816

See no 28.

1819

"Passenger List of the Ship 'Elizabeth,' Which Arrived at Philadelphia in 1819," *The Pennsylvania Magazine of History and Biography* xxv (1901) 255–258   **192**

    Copied from the original in the Library of the Historical Society of Pennsylvania.
    Contains 83 names and contractual obligations of both the passengers and the captain, concluding "Amsterdam, 4 May, 1819."

DELAWARE

1641

G. B. Keen, "The Third Swedish Expedition to New Sweden," *The Pennsylvania Magazine of History and Biography* III (1879) 462–464 **193**

From copies in the Historical Society of Pennsylvania of originals in the Royal Archives at Stockholm.

Names of emigrants who embarked on the *Kalmar Nyckel* and *Charitas* for New Sweden in 1641.

Intended to accompany an article by C. T. Odhner, "The Founding of New Sweden, 1637–1642," on p 269–284, 395–411 of the same volume.

1649

G. B. Keen, "The Eighth Swedish Expedition to New Sweden," *The Pennsylvania Magazine of History and Biography* VIII (1884) 107–108 **194**

From a copy in the Historical Society of Pennsylvania of the original in the Royal Archives in Stockholm.

List of persons, male and female, who set out with Commandant Hans Amundson for New Sweden July 3 1649.

1661

Louis P. de Boer, "Delaware Papers. Passenger List of Colonists to the South River (Delaware) Colony of New Netherland, 1661," *The New York Genealogical and Biographical Record* LX (1929) 68–70 **195**

Two lists, the first undated and containing the names of 15 "Colonists and other Freemen who have already applied for going to the Colony of this City in New Netherland," the second comprising the passenger list of "De Purmerender Kerck" which sailed from Texel Nov 24 1661 for New Amstel, Delaware. Photostat illustration of original list taken from Old City Archives, Amsterdam.

See note for no 196.

1661–1662

A. R. Dunlap, "Three Lists of Passengers to New Amstel," *Delaware History* VIII (1959) 310–311 **196**

Transcribed from a microfilm copy in the Historical Society of Delaware from ms records in the Archives of the city of Amsterdam. Contains 3 lists giving the names of 37 persons or families bound for the Delaware River area on the *Purmerlander Kerck* (Purmerland Church) and the *Gulden Arent* (Golden Eagle).

The initial list of the *Purmerlander Kerck*, dated here "November 13, 1661," also printed in no 195.

1662

"Emigrants to the Colonie on the Delaware River. List of the Colonists and Other Free People Who Have Entered to Go to This City's Colonie

Delaware, 1662, continued

in New Netherland" (*In* Edmund Bailey O'Callaghan *Documents Relative to the Colonial History of the State of New York,* Albany, Weed, Parsons & Co 1858, ɪɪ 183)   *197*

A list of 38 persons who contracted with the authorities of the city of Amsterdam to emigrate to the colony on the Delaware River.

1803–1806

See no 25.

MARYLAND

1633

" 'The Ark' and 'The Dove' " (*In* John Jacob Raskob *Raskob-Green Record Book* Claymont, Delaware 1921, p 95–97)　　**198**
The passengers with Governor Leonard Calvert.
Also printed in *198A*, "Documented List of the Adventures on the Ark and the Dove and Those Who were Early Identified with the Settlement," in Harry Wright Newman, *The flowering of the Maryland Palatinate* (Washington, The Author 1961) p 339–341; *198B* J. Moss Ives, *The Ark and The Dove* (London, Longmans, Green and Co 1936) p 110; *198C* Edward D. Neill, *The Founders of Maryland* (Albany, Joel Munsell 1876) p 64; *198D* Hester Dorsey Richardson, *Side-Lights on Maryland History with Sketches of Early Maryland Families* (Baltimore, Williams & Wilkins Co 1913) i 9–15, 411–418; *198E* J. Thomas Scharf, *History of Maryland from the Earliest Period to the Present Day* (Baltimore, John Piet 1879) i 66.

1646–1775

See no 10.

1654–1686

Gordon Ireland, "Servants to Foreign Plantations from Bristol, England, 1654–1686," *The New York Genealogical and Biographical Record* LXXIX (1948) 65–75　　**199**
An extract from no 11 of 155 servants bound for Maryland, 3 for New York (1678), 17 for Pennsylvania (1684–1685), and 2 for Virginia (1675–1677).
Names arranged chronologically under colony, with only location in "Servants to Foreign Plantations," the ms source volume.
Main list followed by table of bondmasters, table of ships and ship masters, and table of places from which the emigrants came.

1666–1750

[Names of aliens naturalized by special acts of the Provincial Legislature, 1666–1750] (*In* J. Thomas Scharf *History of Maryland from the Earliest Period to the Present Day*, Baltimore, John B. Piet 1879, ii 11)　　**200**
List of 175 foreigners naturalized in Maryland during the period covered. Gives name only.
Also printed in part in *200A* "Early Maryland Naturalization, Etc., from Kilty's Laws," in Gaius Marcus Brumbaugh, *Maryland Records, Colonial, Revolutionary, County and Church* (Lancaster, Lancaster Press, Inc 1928) p 311–313.

1683–1684

See no 12.

1686

See no 220.

Maryland, continued

1697–1707

See no 14.

1714

[Passengers on the *American Merchant*, 1714] (*In* Edward Duffield Neill *Terra Mariae; or Threads of Maryland Colonial History*, Philadelphia, J. B. Lippincott & Co 1867, p 202)   **201**

From a letter from a Glasgow merchant, dated Jan 19 1714 and addressed to "Mr. Thomas Mackey, merch't on Potomoak River," in the possession of a relative of the author.

Gives the names and occupations of 17 men and boys who shipped on the *American Merchant*, 1714.

1716

"A List of Rebbells Transported in the Shipp *Friendship* of Belfast, Michael Mankin, Comander, the 20ᵗʰ of August, 1716" (*In* J. Thomas Scharf *History of Maryland from the Earliest Period to the Present Day*, Baltimore, John B. Piet 1879 ɪ 386–387)   **202**

The names of 80 political prisoners, mostly Scotchmen deported after the defeat of Mar and Derwentwater's rising in 1715–1716, with names of purchasers. Taken from a proclamation in the Public Record Office, London.

Also printed in **202A** Hester Dorsey Richardson, *Side-Lights on Maryland History with Sketches of Early Maryland Families* (Baltimore, Williams & Wilkins Co 1913) p 215.

"A List of the Rebell prisoners transported into this province in the Ship *Good Speed*, on the 18th Day of October, Anno Domini 1716, with the names of the persons who purchased them" (*In* J. Thomas Scharf *History of Maryland from the Earliest Period to the Present Day*, Baltimore, John B. Piet 1879 ɪ 388–389)   **203**

A list of 55 Scottish prisoners, taken from the same source as no 202.

Also printed in **203A** Hester Dorsey Richardson, *Side-Lights on Maryland History with Sketches of Early Maryland Families* (Baltimore, Williams & Wilkins 1913) p 24.

1740

Frank F. White, Jr, "A List of Convicts Transported to Maryland," *Maryland Historical Magazine* xLɪɪɪ (1948) 55–60   **204**

From a document in the Maryland Historical Society.

P 57–59 contain "A List of One Hundred and Fifteen Felons & Convicts Shipped from Newgate by Andrew Reid Esqr on Board the York Capt Anthony Bacon Commander, bound for Maryland."

Gives name only.

1747

[Scotch prisoners deported to Maryland on the ship *Johnson*, 1747] (*In* J. Thomas Scharf *History of Maryland from the Earliest Period to the Present Day*, Baltimore, John B. Piet 1879, ɪ 435) **205**

From a certified list among the records at Annapolis.

The names of 96 Scottish prisoners taken after the battle of Culloden who were shipped to Maryland on the *Johnson* of Liverpool, William Pemberton, master, arriving at the port of Oxford on July 20 1747.

1767–1772

"Naturalization of Maryland Settlers in Pennsylvania," *Maryland Historical Magazine* v (1910) 72 **206**

The names of 23 Marylanders, probably Dunkers or Mennonites, who went to Pennsylvania for naturalization in the latter days of the Province, most of them being naturalized at York.

1798

Kate Singer Curry, "Naturalizations — during the Court Sessions of January, 1798, Washington Co., Maryland," *National Genealogical Society Quarterly* xxɪɪɪ (1935) 111–113 **207**

The names of 45 aliens naturalized, with their professions and the countries to which they were formerly subject.

1811

See no 27.

1815–1816

See no 28.

VIRGINIA

1607–1616

Robert Armistead Stewart, "Ancient Planters" (*In* Nell Marion Nugent *Cavaliers and Pioneers; Abstracts of Virginia Land Patents and Grants, 1623–1800.* Richmond, Dietz Printing co 1934, I xxviii–xxxiv) **208**

A list of those known to have come to Virginia before the close of 1616, with date of arrival and ship supplied when known.

Cavaliers and Pioneers was reissued in facsimile by the Genealogical Publishing Co, Baltimore, 1963.

1607–1623

"Lists of the Livinge & the Dead in Virginia February 16, 1623" (In *Colonial Records of Virginia.* Richmond, R. F. Walker, Superintendent of Public Printing 1874, p 33–66) **208-1**

Published by the Joint Committee on Library (Senate Document, Extra) under the chairmanship of Thomas H. Wynne and W. S. Gilman.

From a copy obtained by Colonel Angus W. McDonald from the Public Record Office, London.

Pages 37–54 contain "A List of the Livinge"; p 55–60 contain "A List of the Names of the Dead in Virginia Since April Last. Feby 16th, 1623"; p 61–66 contain a list of those massacred by the Indians on Mar 22 1622.

Gives name only, arranged under place of residence.

Contains many more names than the census of 1624/25 given in no 210.

1607–1624

"Census of Inhabitants: Names of the First Settlers at Jamestown, 1607; Names of Those Who Came in the First Supply; Names of Those Who Came in the Second Supply; Names of Inhabitants of Jamestown in 1624" (*In* Lyon Gardiner Tyler *The Cradle of the Republic: Jamestown and James River,* Richmond, The Hermitage Press 1906, p 100–104) **209**

Taken from *Capt. John Smith, of Willoughby by Alfred, Lincolnshire . . . Works 1608–1631 . . . Edited by Edward Arber* (Birmingham 1884, *The English Scholar's Library No. 16*) p 389–390, 411–412, 445–446, and from no 1, p 173–178.

No ship mentioned.

For a useful tabulation of arrival dates of ships coming to Virginia, 1607–1624, see Addams Stratton McAllister, "Tabulation Showing Ships Which Delivered in Virginia Persons Still Living There at the Taking of the Official Census in 1624/5," *National Genealogical Society Quarterly* XIV (1925) 23.

1607–1625

"Musters of the Inhabitants in Virginia 1624/1625" (*In* Annie Lash Jester and Martha Woodroof Hiden *Adventurers of Purse and Person; Virginia, 1607–1625,* Princeton, Princeton University Press 1956, p 5–69) **210**

Virginia, 1607–1625, continued

From the original preserved in the State Papers of the Public Record Office, London. The document has never before been printed in full.

A census of the inhabitants of Virginia taken between 20 Jan and 7 Feb 1624/25. Contains 1,232 names, with the age of each person and the ship in which he arrived frequently indicated.

See note for no 208–1.

1610–1629

"Burgesses of the Assembly Convened at Jamestown, October 16, 1629" (*In* Edward Duffield Neill *Virginia Carolorum: The Colony under the Rule of Charles the First and Second, A. D. 1625-A. D. 1685, Based upon Manuscripts and Documents of the Period*, Albany, Joel Munsell's Sons 1886, p 71–74) **211**

Names 44 legislators of early Virginia, giving dates of arrival into the Colony, the ships in which they came, and their ages at the time of assembly.

1618–1623

"Muster of the Inhabitants in Virginia. Taken in 1625. Total, 1,095. The Muster of the Inhabitants at Wariscoyack, Taken the 7th of February, 1625," *William and Mary College Quarterly Historical Magazine* vii (1899) 217–218 **212**

From Isle of Wight county records.

Several short lists of emigrants to Virginia, 1618–1623, with name, age, ship and year of arrival given.

Also printed in no 210.

1620–1621

Winifred Lovering Holman, "Marriages of Emigrants to Virginia," *The Virginia Magazine of History and Biography* xl (1932) 80 **213**

List of five couples from Isle of Wight parish register married just before leaving for Virginia.

1621–1623

"Mr. Danniell Gookines Muster" (*In* Frederick William Gookin *Daniel Gookin, 1612–1687*, Chicago, F. W. Gookin 1912, p 47–48) **214**

Twenty servants transported to Newport News in the *Flying Hart*, 1621, and the *Providence*, 1623.

Gives name and age only.

Also printed in **214A** Aubrey Gwynn, "Documents Relating to the Irish in the West Indies," *Analecta Hibernia* iv (1932) 165–166, and in no 210.

1623

"Minutes of the Council and General Court, 1622–1624," *The Virginia Magazine of History and Biography* xix 113–148 **215**

From the originals in the Library of Congress.

Pages 131–134 contain lists of English emigrants who arrived on the *Ann* and *Benny Bess* before Feb 1623.

1623–1666

George Cabell Greer, *Early Virginia Immigrants* (Richmond, W. C. Hill Printing Co 1912) 376 p **216**

Contains 25,000 names collected from the records of the Virginia State Land Office, 1623–1666.

Excerpts of the Irish names from this list were published in **216A** Michael J. O'Brien, "Early Immigrants to Virginia (1623 to 1666) Collected by George Cabell Greer, Clerk, Virginia State Land Office, from the Records of the Land Office, in Richmond," *The Journal of the American Irish Historical Society* XIII (1914) 209–213.

No ship mentioned.

Reprinted in facsimile by the Genealogical Publishing Co, Baltimore, 1960.

1635

H. G. Somerby, "Passengers for Virginia, 1635," *The New England Historical and Genealogical Register* II (1848) 111–113, 211–212, 268, 374–375; III (1849) 184, 388–390; IV (1850) 61, 189–191, 261–264; V (1851) 61–62, 343–344; XV (1861) 142–146 **217**

From original records of the Master of Rolls, London.

Gives name and age only.

1635–1800

William Glover Stanard, *Some Emigrants to Virginia: Memoranda in Regard to Several Hundred Emigrants to Virginia During the Colonial Period Whose Parentage is Shown or Former Residence Indicated by Authentic Records* (Richmond, The Bell Book and Stationery Co 1915) 94 p **218**

"Second edition, enlarged." Much more complete than the first edition published in 1911.

An alphabetical list of emigrants to Virginia, 1635–1800, culled from a variety of sources.

No ship mentioned.

Reissued in facsimile by the Genealogical Book Co, Baltimore, 1953.

1636–1637

Martha W. Hiden, ed, "Accompts of the Tristram and Jane," *The Virginia Magazine of History and Biography* LXII (1954) 424–447 **219**

An account book of an early trading voyage to Virginia found in the Public Record Office, London. Gives the names of 2 paying passengers and of 74 others sold as indentured servants, as well as goods sent back from Virginia on the return voyage. The subsequent history of a number of passengers is traced in the text which follows the account. Photostat illustration of the first page of the *Accompts*.

Virginia, continued

1646–1775

See no 10.

1675–1677

See no 199.

1683–1684

See no 12.

1686

R. Sharpe France, "Early Emigrants to America from Liverpool," *The Genealogists' Magazine* xii (1955–1958) 234–235   **220**
> From a ms in the Lancashire Record Office, County Hall, Preston.
> Names of 34 Persons of Liverpool who indentured themselves for a four-year period of service in Virginia or Maryland, 1686.
> No ship mentioned.

1697–1707

See no 14.

1700

"A List of Ye French Refugees That Are Settled att Mannachin Town. . ." (*In* William Macfarlane Jones, ed *The Douglas Register, Being a Detailed Record of Birth, Marriages and Deaths together with Other Interesting Notes, as Kept by the Rev. William Douglas, from 1750 to 1797*, Richmond, J. W. Fergusson & Sons 1928, p 369–371)   **221**
> Contains 79 names of families or individuals.
> Also printed in no 224.
> No ship mentioned.

"Communication from Governor Francis Nicholson of Virginia Regarding Huguenot Refugees on Board Ship 'Mary and Ann'," *The Huguenot* vi (1933) 82–86   **222**
> Contains a list of refugees who sailed from London on the *Mary and Ann* and arrived at the mouth of the James River on July 23 1700.

Mrs Grant E. Lilly, "Passengers on the *Peter and Anthony*," *The Huguenot* vii (1933–1935) 153–155   **223**
> Contains a "List of All Ye Passingers from London to James River in Virginia, Being French Refugees Imbarqued in the Ship Ye Peter and Anthony, Galley of London, Daniel Perreau Commander."
> Also printed in no 224.

1700–1714

R. A. Brock, *Documents, Chiefly Unpublished, Relating to the Huguenot Emigration to Virginia and to the Settlement at Manakin-Town, with an Appendix of Genealogies, Presenting Data on the Fontaine, Maury, Dupuy,*

Trabue, Marye, Chastain, Cocke and Other Families (Richmond, Virginia Historical Society 1886) 247 p **224**

New Series Volume v of the *Collections of the Virginia Historical Society.*

Contains a number of lists of refugees and immigrants and several passenger lists, including that of the *Peter and Anthony* which landed 170 refugees in Jamestown in Sept 1700.

Reissued in facsimile by the Genealogical Publishing Co, Baltimore, 1962.

1707

"Immigrant List, 1707" (*In* William Fletcher Boogher *Gleanings of Virginia History,* Washington, D C, W. F. Boogher 1903, p 8) **225**

Eighteen persons who shipped at Bristol, England, in the *Joseph and Thomas* and received wages as deck hands.

1714

"Liste Generalle de Tous les Francois Protestants Refugies Establys dans la Paroisse du Roy Guillaume d'Henrico en Virginia, y Compres les Femmes, Enfans, Veuses, et Orphelins" (*In* William Macfarlane Jones *The Douglas Register, Being a Detailed Record of Births, Marriages and Deaths together with Other Interesting Notes, as Kept by the Rev. William Douglas, from 1750 to 1797,* Richmond, J. W. Fergusson & Sons 1928, p 372–374) **226**

Date is approximate.

Reprinted from **226A** William Stevens Perry, *Papers Relating to the History of the Church in Virginia, A. D. 1650–1776* (Hartford, Privately Printed 1870) p 193–195. Also printed in no 224.

1735–1757

"Importations" (*In* William Wallace Scott *A History of Orange County Virginia,* Richmond, Everett Waddey Co 1907, p 225–229) **227**

A list of persons who imported themselves or were imported as servants by others and who later proved their importation to obtain their "head rights" to land in the colony. Date shows year proof was made and recorded.

List compiled by Philip H. Fry, Clerk of County and Circuit Courts.

No ship mentioned.

A History of Orange County, Virginia was reprinted in facsimile by the Chesapeake Book Co, Berryville, Va, 1962.

1739–1740

Mrs W. W. King, "Augusta County Early Settlers, Importations, 1739–1740," *National Genealogical Society Quarterly* xxv (1937) 46–48 **228**

A list of Augusta County settlers who proved their importations from Great Britain at their own expense in order to become entitled to enter public land. These proceedings were before the Orange County Court.

Also printed in **228A** "Importations, 1739–1740," in Oren F. Morton, *A History of Rockbridge County, Virginia,* Staunton, Va, The McClure Co 1920, p 756–757, and in no 227.

DISTRICT OF COLUMBIA

1802–1850

Vivian Holland Jewett, "Abstracts of Naturalization Records, Circuit Court, District of Columbia," *National Genealogical Society Quarterly* XLI (1953) 41–44, 90–92, 130–131; XLII (1954) 22–24, 68–73, 149–150; XLIII (1955) 20–21, 146–147; XLIV (1956) 16–19, 109–111, 147–149; XLV (1957) 21–26

229

From records of the Circuit Court, District of Columbia, now in the National Archives, Washington.

An alphabetical list of petitions received before the Court, giving name, age, year of petition, nativity, place from which petitioner emigrated, place where he arrived, names of witnesses, and date of naturalization. Includes entries to all ports of the Atlantic coast.

Divided into 2 sections: Petitions Received, 1802–1820; Petitions Received, 1821–1850.

Apparently incomplete; published only through "Petitions Received, 1817[1821]–1850," the name "Law."

No ship mentioned.

NORTH CAROLINA
1683–1684

See no 12.

1695–1702

William J. Gammon, "Emigrants to Bath County, North Carolina, 1695–1702," *National Genealogical Society Quarterly* xxv (1937) 28–30   **230**

From an old deed book in Craven County, N C.

A chronological list of emigrants brought to Bath County, N C, for which land was granted to the person bringing them or inducing them to come.

No ship mentioned.

1706–1795

See no 131.

1709

See no 16.

1709–1710

See no 144.

1728–1771

See nos 147 and 175.

1753–1759

[Lists of Moravian immigrants to North Carolina, 1753–1759] (*In* Adelaide L. Fries *Records of the Moravians in North Carolina*, Raleigh, Edwards & Broughman Printing Co 1922, ɪ 68–69, 73–74)   **231**

Two lists, the first giving 26 names of Moravian immigrants to North Carolina between 1753–1759 made up from certificates of land grants in the Herrnhut (Saxony) archives; the second being a list of colonists sent to North Carolina in 1753. First list gives name and former city of residence in Europe only; second list gives name, age nationality, and occupation of each immigrant.

No ship mentioned.

1774–1775

A. R. Newsome, ed, *Records of Emigrants from England and Scotland to North Carolina, 1774–1775* (Raleigh, State Department of Archives and History 1962) 30 p   **232**

Compiled from transcripts in the North Carolina Historical Commission of original lists in the Public Record Office, London.

Reprinted from **232A** *The North Carolina Historical Review* xɪ (Jan 1934) 39–54, (Apr 1934) 129–143.

Also printed in part in no 21.

SOUTH CAROLINA
1679

"Foreign Protestants for Carolina in 1679," *Proceedings of the Huguenot Society of London* x (1912–1914) 187–189   **233**

From records of the Admiralty now preserved in the Public Record Office.

Two lists, one of 67 persons going to Carolina in the *Richmond*, the other of 90 French Protestants willing to be transported to the Ashley River region of South Carolina.

Also printed in **233A** St Julien R. Childs, "The Petit-Guérard Colony," *The South Carolina Historical and Genealogical Magazine* XLIII (1942) 1–2.

1683–1684

See no 12.

1695–1696

Daniel Ravenel, *"Liste des François et Suisses" from an Old Manuscript List of French and Swiss Protestants Settled in Charleston, on the Santee and at the Orange Quarter in Carolina Who Desired Naturalization. Prepared Probably about 1695–6* (New York, The Knickerbocker Press 1888) 77 p   **234**

From a ms in the possession of the author.

Contains a list of 154 French and Swiss refugees who declared themselves willing to be naturalized in anticipation of the act of naturalization of 1696. Gives name and origin.

Originally published in the *Southern Intelligencer*, a religious weekly newspaper of Charleston, in June 1822.

1706–1795

See no 131.

1709

See no 16.

1728

Theodore D. Jervey, "The White Indentured Servants of South Carolina," *The South Carolina Historical and Genealogical Magazine* XII (1911) 163–171   **235**

P 171 contains a "List of Convicts Imported from Bristol to the province of S° Carolina on board the Ship called the Expedition. . . ," giving 24 names with date and place of conviction and term of imprisonment.

1728–1771

See nos 147 and 175.

South Carolina, continued

1732

Henry A. M. Smith, "Purrysburgh," *The South Carolina Historical and Genealogical Magazine* x (1909) 187–219   **236**

P 208–210 contains "A List of the Germains and Switz Protestants under the Command of Coll° Purry qualified before his Excellency Robert Johnson Esquire Governour of this Province on the 22 and 23 days of December 1732," being the names of 93 alien settlers naturalized on those days. Gives name and age only.

1742–1749

Gilbert P. Voigt, "The German and German-Swiss Element in South Carolina, 1732–1752," *Bulletin of the University of South Carolina* cxiii (1922) 60 p   **237**

On p 56–60 is contained a list of 136 German or German-Swiss settlers at Saxe-Gotha, or Congaree, arranged according to date of grant of land, with place of origin frequently given.

No ship mentioned.

1763–1773

Janie Revill, *A Compilation of the Original Lists of Protestant Immigrants to South Carolina, 1763–1773* (Columbia, The State Co 1939) 163 p **238**

Transcribed from the *Journals* of the Council of the Colony of South Carolina.

Gives name of immigrant only and the number of acres of land allotted to him under the Bounty Act of 1761.

Contains an index of names.

1774–1775

See no 21.

GEORGIA

1732

E. Merton Coulter, ed, "A List of the First Shipload of Georgia Settlers," *Georgia Historical Quarterly* xxxi (1947) 282–288   **239**

A list by Capt Thomas of the *Anne* of persons sent to Georgia in Nov 1732 for the purpose of establishing the Colony there. Meticulously annotated to furnish information on the subsequent careers of these original settlers. Contains 118 names.

1732–1742

E. Merton Coulter and Albert B. Saye, eds, *A List of the Early Settlers of Georgia* (Athens, The University of Georgia Press 1949) 103 p   **240**

From a ms volume in the University of Georgia Library.

Contains the names of approximately 2,800 emigrants to Georgia between June 1732 and June 1742 arranged under two headings: Persons Who Went from Europe to Georgia at the Trustees' Charge, and Persons Who Went from Europe to Georgia on Their Own Account.

Names grouped alphabetically under each division, with age, occupation, date of embarkation, and date of arrival given.

No ship mentioned.

1734–1741

See no 144.

1735–1775

"Arrivals in Georgia" (*In* Adelaide L. Fries *The Moravians in Georgia, 1735–1740*. Raleigh, N C, The Author 1905, p 236–238)   **240-1**

The names of 47 foreigners who emigrated to Georgia, 1734–1775, with country of origin given.

1774–1775

See no 21.

FLORIDA

1538–1559

Spain. Archivo General de Indias, Seville. *Catálogo de Pasajeros a Indias durante los Siglos* xvi, xvii *y* xviii *Redactado por el Personal Facultativo del Archivo General de Indias bajo la Dirección del Director del Mismo Don Cristóbal Bermúdez Plata* (Sevilla, Imprenta Editorial de la Gavidia 1940–1946) 3 vols **241**

From documents in the Archivo covering the period 1509–1790.

Vol i, 1509–1534; vol ii, 1535–1538; vol iii, 1539–1559. Vol i supersedes an ed covering the years 1509–1533 published at the expense of La Inspección General de Emigración del Ministerio de Trabajo y Previsión (Madrid, Imprenta Espasa-Calpe, S. A. 1930).

A chronological list of passengers en route to Spanish America (including Florida and Louisiana between 1538–1559).

Gives name of emigrant, place of origin, date of departure, destination, and master of the ship on which he sailed.

Contains an index of names, a geographical index giving places of origin and destination, and an index of ship masters.

No ship mentioned.

LOUISIANA

1538–1559

See no 241.

1718–1724

"Ship Lists of Passengers Leaving France for Louisiana, 1718–1724," *The Louisiana Historical Quarterly* xiv (1931) 516–520; xv (1932) 68–77, 453– 467; xxi (1938) 965–978 **242**

"Transcribed from the copies of the originals obtained in France for the Louisiana Historical Society, now in its library in the Cabildo in New Orleans in a bound volume entitled 'Louisiane. Passagers. 1718–1724'." Translated by Albert Laplace Dart. Introduction by Henry P. Dart.

The fourth installment carries through the period ending Apr 11 1720. No further installments have appeared after it and, according to a past editor, none have been included in the unpublished numbers of the *Quarterly* for the period July 1951 – Jan 1955, now in ms.

1797

L. Perez, "French Immigrants to Louisiana 1796–1800," *Publications of the Southern History Association* xi (1907) 106–112 **242-1**

A list, extracted from official documents and correspondence, of 99 persons emigrating from France to Louisiana in 1797.

Gives name and age only.

1813–1837

Mrs F. O. James, "Passenger Lists Taken from Manifests of the Customs Service, Port of New Orleans, 1813–1837," *New Orleans Genesis* i (1962) 23–28 **243**

A chronological list of passengers who landed at New Orleans during the period covered. Gives name of vessel and passenger and date of entry into the manifest book.

To be contined; vol i no 1 (Jan 1962) records the years 1813–1821 only.

Appendix I

Published Lists of Ship Passengers and Immigrants after 1825

THE FOLLOWING are references to published lists of ship passengers and immigrants coming to North America after 1825 (and usually before 1900) which turned up during searches for lists in the pre-1825 period. They are included here because of their obvious usefulness to genealogists and historians and as a possible point of departure for anyone who may wish to attempt to compile a more comprehensive list of them. No claim is made for completeness; indeed, they represent merely random discoveries, and it is quite likely that many more are scattered about between the covers of genealogical and historical tomes. For the most part, emigrants arriving in America after 1825 almost immediately journeyed inland, and authors, compilers and editors who have reported such lists have usually been more concerned with the final point of settlement than with the port at which these immigrants arrived. Consequently, these references are grouped under the earliest date of entry and not geographically, as the earlier lists are arranged.

R. J. W.

1823–1890

"Tabelle der Auswanderer des 19. Jahrhunderts" (*In* Robert Mörsdorf *Die Auswanderung aus dem Birkenfelder Land*. Bonn, Ludwig Röhrscheid Verlag 1939, p 96–174)　　**244**

An alphabetical register of emigrants from the principality of Birkenfeld during the 19th century, giving date of departure and point of destination, most frequently America. Includes a few emigrants between 1823 and 1825.

1827–1898

Hewitt L. Foryth and Ervin Peter Smith, Sr, "Naturalization Record Index, New Orleans, Louisiana," *New Orleans Genesis* i (1962) 4–7, 120–124, 221–226　　**245**

An index of persons naturalized in New Orleans during the period covered. Names arranged alphabetically according to their respective volumes.

1830

Mary P. Lord, "Passenger List, Liverpool, England, 1830," *The New England Historical and Genealogical Register* xciii (1939) 298–300 **246**

Contains the names of 109 passengers who sailed from Liverpool England in 1830 on the *Mexico*, Actor P. Patterson of Kennebunkport, Me, captain. The original list is in the possession of the author, a granddaughter of Captain Patterson.

Gives name, former place of residence, nationality, age, occupation, and height of each immigrant.

1832

Fritz Braun, "Auswanderer auf dem Schiff 'Elizabeth' Bremen-New York 1832," *Mitteilungen zur Wanderungsgeschichte der Pfälzer (Beilage zu Pfälzische Familien- und Wappenkunde)* folge 9 (1957) 61–68 **247**

From the original list in the National Archives, Washington.

Contains the names of emigrants from the Palatine — including many Mennonites — and groups them under village or town from whence they came. Gives name and age of each emigrant and of his family and frequently identifies the area where he settled.

1832–1849

Friedrich Spengemann, *Die Reisen der Segelfregatten "Isabella" "Pauline" "Meta" und "Uhland" nach Nordamerika. Nach Kapitän Jürgen Meyers Bordbuch* (Bremen, Buchdruckerei Vahland & Co 1937) 136 p **248**

Contains lists of passengers on the *Isabella*, 1832–1839, the *Pauline*, 1839–1842, the *Meta*, 1842, and the *Uhland*, 1849, bound between Bremen and New York or Breman and New Orleans.

Gives name, age, and place of origin.

1832–1903

Fritz Braun, *Auswanderer aus der Mennonitegemeinde Friedsheim im 19. Jahrhundert* (Ludwigshafen am Rhein, Richard Louis Verlag 1956) 28 p **249**

Heft 1 of *Schriften zur Wanderungsgeschichte der Pfälzer.*

An alphabetical list of Mennonites from the area of Friedelsheim during the period covered, giving place and date of birth of each emigrant and of his family and the area where he eventually settled.

Reprinted from *Mitteilungen zur Wanderungsgeschichte der Pfälzer (Beilage zu Pfälzische Familien- und Wappenkunde)* folge 1–4 (1955) 1–16, 17–28.

1833

Fritz Braun, "Auswanderer auf dem Schiff 'Logan' Le Havre-New York 1833," *Mitteilungen zur Wanderungsgeschichte der Pfälzer (Beilage zu Pfälzische Familien- und Wappenkunde)* folge 10 (1957) 69–76 **250**

From the original list in the National Archives, Washington.

The passenger list of the *Logan* which sailed from Le Havre on May 1 1833 and landed at New York on June 20. Contains 132 passengers alphabetically arranged.

Gives name of emigrant, his age, occupation, and geographical origin, and frequently identifies the place where he settled.

1834

[Passenger manifest of the ship *Atlantic*, 1834] (In *The Story of Sloanes*. New York, W. & J. Sloane 1950, p 9)   251

Photostat illustration of the custom record of the Port of New York, probably now in the National Archives, Washington.

Gives 73 names, together with age, sex, occupation, the country of origin, and the country of intended settlement for each passenger.

1836

Louis C. Cramton, "Passenger List of the 'Sarah Sheaffe', May, 1836," *The Detroit Society for Genealogical Research Magazine* v (1942) 208   252

A copy of a list attached to a letter from Robert Taylor of Philadelphia to Messrs Abraham Bell & Co, New York, and postmarked "Phila 8 Jul." in the possession of the author.

Lists 60 passengers arriving at Philadelphia from Belfast via New York, May 1836, together with the charges for their baggage.

John J. Raven, "Families in Fressingfield, Eng., 1836, Wishing to Emigrate to America," *The New England Historical and Genealogical Register* XLIX (1895) 337–338   253

From parish records of Fressingfield, Suffolk, England.

A list of 35 persons who were loaned money by the parish for the purpose of emigrating to America. Gives name and age only.

No ship mentioned.

1836–1837

Henry J. Cadbury, "Four Immigrant Shiploads of 1836 and 1837," *The Norwegian-American Historical Association Studies and Records* II (1927) 20–52   254

From documents formerly in the New York Customs House, now in the National Archives, Washington.

Contains a total of 342 passengers on the *Norden, den Norske Klippe, Aegir* and *Enigheden* which arrived in New York in 1836 and 1837.

Gives name, age, sex, and occupation of each passenger.

1840

C. A. Clausen, "An Immigrant Shipload of 1840," *Norwegian-American Studies and Records* XIV (1944) 54–77   255

P 63–64 contain a manifest of passengers on board the ship *Emelie* which sailed from Drammen for Göteborg en route to New York where it arrived on Aug 12 1840.

Published Lists of Ship Passengers and Immigrants after 1825, continued

From a document formerly in the archives of the New York Customs House, now in the National Archives, Washington.

Contains 89 names, with the age, sex, occupation, and country of origin of each emigrant, and the country of intended settlement ("Missouri" indicated for the majority of passengers).

1840–1860

Joseph Scheben, *Untersuchungen zur Methode und Technik der Deutsch-amerikanischen Wanderungsforschung an Hand eines Vergleichs der Volkszählungslisten der Township Westphalia, Clinton County, Michigan, vom Jahre 1860 mit Auswanderungsakten des Kreises Adenau (Rhineland); mit Mehreren Tabellen, Diagrammen, Kartenskizzen und Kartogrammen, sowie einem Text- und Briefanhang* (Bonn, Ludwig Röhrscheid Verlag 1939) 155 p, 4 tables **256**

Heft 3 of *Forschungen zur Rheinischen Auswanderung.*

A study of emigration from Adenau to America during the period covered as shown through a comparison of a census of Westphalia Township, Clinton County, Michigan, taken in 1860, with emigration acts of Adenau from 1840 on.

Gives name and national origin of all residents of the township in 1860 and name and place of birth of all immigrants from Adenau.

No ship mentioned.

1842

Lucy Mary Kellogg, "Ship List of the *Orient,* 19 May 1842," *The Detroit Society for Genealogical Research Magazine* xxvi (1962) 63–64 **257**

From records of the Port of New York in the National Archives, Washington.

One hundred and eighty-eight passengers on the *Orient* which left Falmouth, England, May 19 1842 destined for New York. Contains name, age, and occupation of each emigrant.

1847–1855

Eilish Ellis, "State-Aided Emigration Schemes from Crown Estates in Ireland c. 1850," *Analecta Hibernica* xxii (1960) 329–394 **258**

From documents in the Quit Rent Office, Dublin.

P 339–347 contain a list of emigrants from Ballykilcline to New York via Dublin and Liverpool, 1847–1848; p 354–367 contain emigrants from Irvilloughter and Boughhill to New York and Quebec, 1848–1849; p 372–379 list emigrants from Kingwilliamstown Estate to New York via Cork and Liverpool, 1849–1855; p 382 contains the names of emigrants from Castlemaine to New York via Liverpool, 1848–1851; and p 384–385 emigrants from Kilconcouse to New York via Dublin and Liverpool, 1852.

Gives name, age, occupation, place of settlement, date of departure, and date of arrival for each emigrant.

1850

"Passenger List of Ship 'Catherine,'" *Michigan Heritage* ii (1960) 15–16
259

A list of 29 passengers sailing from Amsterdam to New York, August 14 – Sept 17 1850, giving age, birthplace, and occupation of each emigrant. They afterwards migrated to Kalamazoo, Mich.

From a letter given to Messrs L. Hensen & Co, Amsterdam, by Anna B. den Bleyker, a relative of one of the passengers.

1850–1882

Karl Friedrich von Frank, "Auswanderer aus Goisern nach Nordamerika 1850 bis 1882," *Senftenegger Monatsblatt für Genealogie und Heraldik* III (1955–1956) 233–240 **260**

An alphabetical list of emigrants from the Austrian village of Goisern to America during the period covered. Gives name, birth date, and date of departure.

No ship mentioned.

1857–1889

J. Walterscheid, *Auswanderer aus dem Siegkreis* (Bonn, Ludwig Röhrscheid Verlag 1939) 104 p **261**

Heft 2 of *Forschungen zur Rheinischen Auswanderung.*

From documents in the Staatsarchiv, Düsseldorf.

A list of emigrants from the area of the present province of North Rhine-Westphalia during the period covered. Emigrants listed chronologically under the towns and villages from where they departed. Gives name and place and date of birth of each emigrant and of his family and the place of eventual settlement.

No ship mentioned.

1878

"A Passenger List of Mennonite Immigrants from Russia in 1878," *The Mennonite Quarterly Review* xv (1941) 263–276 **262**

From a document in the Mennonite Historical Library at Goshen College.

A list of steerage passengers on the North German Lloyd steamer *Strassburg* from Bremen to New York June 18 1878.

Gives name, place of origin, and place of intended settlement, usually Kansas, Nebraska, Minnesota, or Dakota.

Appendix II

Passenger Arrival Records in the National Archives [1]

By FRANK E. BRIDGERS

(Republished in a slightly revised form from the *National Genealogical Society Quarterly* L no 1 September 1962)

PASSENGER LISTS in the National Archives relate to various United States ports on the Atlantic and Gulf of Mexico.[2] Table A shows by name of port or district passenger lists preserved in the National Archives for the period 1819–1945 and the inclusive dates of each type of list. These lists fall within two major groups, customs passenger lists and immigration passenger lists, depending upon whether they were transferred from the Bureau of Customs of the Department of the Treasury or from the Immigration and Naturalization Service of the Department of Justice.

Customs passenger lists, the majority of which have been microfilmed, consist of original lists, copies of lists, abstracts of lists, and State Department transcripts. The original lists were prepared by masters of vessels who were required by federal law to submit to the collectors of customs lists of passengers boarding their vessels at foreign ports. The collectors of customs were then required to furnish quarterly copies or abstracts of the originals to the Secretary of State who was to make a report to Congress at each of its sessions. The transcripts were apparently prepared by the State Department from

[1] The phrase "Passenger Arrival Records" is used here in order to cover not only passenger lists and related indexes but also lists of aliens and cargo manifests.

The examination of passenger arrival records did not extend to records less than 50 years old because of restrictions on their use by the public.

[2] The passenger lists in the National Archives do include a few lists for Great Lakes ports, namely, one for Rochester and a list in duplicate for Sandusky.

There are no passenger arrival records in the National Archives for Pacific Coast ports. A fire of May 4 1851 destroyed records of the port of San Francisco that had accumulated from 1849 when it was established as a port of entry of the United States. A fire of August 18 1940 at Angel Island, California, destroyed lists of passengers arriving in San Francisco, 1851–1936.

copies or abstracts of lists sent to the Secretary of State by the collectors of customs.

As of 1 July 1962 all immigration passenger lists were in the form of negative microfilm only. Positive prints of the rolls reproducing such lists over 50 years old are being prepared for reference purposes. (The rolls reproducing such lists less than 50 years old are not available for reference purposes.)

In addition to customs passenger lists and immigration passenger lists, passenger arrival records in the National Archives include lists of aliens, 1798–1800, for Salem and Beverly, Massachusetts, and cargo manifests, ca 1800–1819, for Alexandria, Virginia, and Philadelphia, and fragmentary manifests for a few other ports for the same period. Some cargo manifests contain names of passengers.

Passenger arrival records in the National Archives also include card indexes to the names on some of the customs passenger lists and card and book indexes to the names on some of the immigration passenger lists. Many of these indexes have been microfilmed. Microfilm copies of the card indexes to the names on some of the immigration passenger lists are occasionally illegible. Table B shows by name of port the dates covered by each type of index. As of 1 July 1962 all card indexes for both customs and immigration passenger lists were in the form of positive microfilm, except for the customs card indexes for the ports of New Bedford, Massachusetts, 1875–1899, and New Orleans, 1900–1902, and the immigration card index for Miami, Florida, 30 December 1929 – 23 February 1942. Of the book indexes to the immigration passenger lists, only those for the port of New York, 1906–1915, had been placed on positive microfilm as of 1 July 1962.

The card indexes to the names on the passenger lists are arranged alphabetically by name of passenger. The book indexes are arranged — with some variations — by name of steamship line, then by date of vessel arrival, and lastly by surname of passenger.

The customs passenger lists and related indexes or microfilm copies of them are available for examination in the search rooms of the National Archives. (When the lists and related indexes are being repaired or microfilmed they are not available for consultation.) As positive microfilm copies of the indexes to the immigration passenger lists are completed, they can likewise be examined in the search rooms of the National Archives provided all entries on each roll relate to lists over 50 years old.

The National Archives will search the customs passenger lists if, in addition to the name of the passenger and the port of entry, the requesting person supplies the name of the vessel and the approximate date of its arrival or the name of the port of embarkation and the exact date of its arrival. It will also search the immigration passenger lists over 50 years old provided the information is needed for genealogical purposes [3] and provided the name of the passenger, the port of entry, the name of the vessel, and the exact date of arrival can be furnished. The National Archives will also examine indexes to the names on the customs passenger lists if the name of the passenger, the port of entry, and the supposed year of arrival can be given. Similarly, it will search the indexes to the immigration passenger lists provided the name of the passenger, the port of entry, and the supposed year of arrival can be given and provided the requested information is needed for genealogical purposes and the relevant indexes are legible.

---

[3] Persons needing information from immigration passenger lists for legal purposes should write to the Immigration and Naturalization Service. Forms for requesting the information are available from the nearest district office of the Service. The locations of district offices can be supplied by any postmaster.

TABLE A

Ports or Districts for Which the National Archives has Passenger Lists, Showing Dates for Each Type of List

Name of port or district [1]	Customs passenger lists			Immigration passenger lists
	Originals	Copies and abstracts	State Dept. transcripts	
Alexandria, Virginia	------	1820-52, 1849	1820-31	------
Annapolis, Maryland	------			------
Apalachicola, Florida	------			Sept. 4, 1918
Baltimore, Maryland	1820-91	1820-69, 1848	1820, 1822-27, 1829	12 Dec. 1891-30 Nov. 1909
Bangor, Maine	------	1820-26	1820-26	------
Barnstable, Massachusetts	------	1825-32, 1867		------
Bath, Maine	------	1865		------
Beaufort, North Carolina	------			------
Belfast, Maine	------	1820-31, 1851	1820, 1822-24, 1827, 1829, 1831	------
Boca Grande, Florida				28 Oct. 1912-16 Aug. 1935
Boston and Charlestown, Mass.[2]	1883-99			
Bridgeport, Connecticut	------	1820-74, 1870	1820-27	1 Aug. 1891-Dec. 1943
Bridgetown, New Jersey	------	1828	1828	------
Bristol and Warren, R. I.	------	1820-24, 1828, 1843-71	1820-28	------
Brunswick, Georgia	------			22 Nov. 1901-27 Nov. 1939
Cape May, New Jersey	------	1828		------
Carabelle, Florida	------			7 Nov. 1915
Charleston, South Carolina[3]	------	1820-29	1820-29	9 Apr. 1906-3 Dec. 1945
Darien, Georgia	------	1823, 1825		------
Delaware (see also entry for Wilmington)			1820	
Dighton, Massachusetts	------	1820-36	1819, 1823, 1826, 1828	------
East River, Virginia	------	1830	1830	------
Edenton, North Carolina	------	1820	1820	------
Edgartown, Massachusetts	------	1820-70	1820-28, 1831-32	------
Fairfield, Connecticut	------	1820-21	1820	------
Fall River, Massachusetts	------	1837-65		------
Fernandina, Florida	------	1821, 1826, 1827	1822, 1825-27	29 Aug. 1904-7 Oct. 1932
Frenchman's Bay, Maine	------	1846-71		------
Galveston, Texas	------	1820-21	1820	------
Georgetown, D. C.	------			------
Georgetown, South Carolina	------			17 June 1923-24 Oct. 1939

Name of port or district	Customs passenger lists			Immigration passenger lists
	Originals	Copies and abstracts	State Dept. transcripts	
Gloucester, Massachusetts		1820, 1832-39, 1867-70		Oct. 1906-June 1923, 1 Feb. 1930-Dec. 1943, Aug. 1904-Sept. 1944
Gulfport, Mississippi		1821		
Hampton, Virginia		1832		
Hartford, Connecticut		1820		Feb. 1929-Dec. 1943
Havre de Grace, Maryland		1852		
Hingham, Massachusetts				
Jacksonville, Florida [4]		1820-27, 1842	1820, 1822-25, 1827	18 Jan. 1904-17 Dec. 1945
Kennebunk, Maine		1837-68		
Key West, Florida				Nov. 1898-Dec. 1945
Knights Key, Florida				7 Feb. 1908-20 Jan. 1912
Little Egg Harbor (port of Tuckerton), New Jersey		1831		
Marblehead, Massachusetts [4]		1820-52	1821-23, 1825-27	
Mayport, Florida [4]				16 Nov. 1907-13 Apr. 1916
Miami, Florida				Oct. 1899-Dec. 1945
Millville, Florida				4 July 1916
Mobile, Alabama	1820-62	1832, 1849-52	1820, 1822-25, 1829, 1831	3 Apr. 1904-24 Dec. 1945
Nantucket, Massachusetts		1820-62		
Newark, New Jersey		1836		
New Bedford, Massachusetts	1823-99	1826-52	1822, 1825-27	1 July 1902-July 1942
New Bern, North Carolina		1820-45, 1865	1830-31	
Newburyport, Massachusetts		1821-39	1820-30	
New Haven, Connecticut		1820-73	1821-31	
New London, Connecticut		1820-47	1822-31	
New Orleans, Louisiana [5]	1820-1902	1820-75	1820, 1823-27, 1829, 1831	Jan. 1903-Dec. 1945
Newport, Rhode Island	1820-97	1820-57	1820-27	
New York, New York		1820-74	1820-28, 1830-31	16 June 1897-1942
Norfolk and Portsmouth, Va		1820-57	1820-27	
Oswegatchie, New York		1821-23	1820-32	
Panama City, Florida			1821-23	10 Nov. 1927-12 Dec. 1939
Pascagoula, Mississippi				15 July 1903-21 May 1935
Passamaquoddy, Maine		1820-59	1822-26, 1831	
Penobscot, Maine		1851		
Pensacola, Florida				12 May, 1900-16 July 1945

Name of port or district	Customs passenger lists			Immigration passenger lists
	Originals	Copies and abstracts	State Dept. transcripts	
Perth Amboy, N. J.		1820, 1829-32	1829	
Petersburg, Virginia	1820-99	1820-21	1819-20, 1822	Jan. 1883-31 Dec. 1945
Philadelphia, Pennsylvania		1820-54	1820-22, 1824-27, 1829, 1822, 1824, 1826-27, 1829-30	
Plymouth, Massachusetts		1821-43		
Plymouth, North Carolina		1820, 1825, 1840	1820, 1823	15 Feb. 1932-10 Dec. 1945
Port Everglades, Florida				29 Mar. 1912-2 Jan. 1913
Port Inglis, Florida			1820-32	Nov. 1893-Mar. 1943
Portland and Falmouth, Maine²		1820-68, 1873		
Port Royal, South Carolina		1865	1820, 1822, 1824-31	12 Jan. 1923-13 Oct. 1939
Portsmouth, New Hampshire		1820-61		June 1911-June 1943
Port St. Joe, Florida		1820-67	1820, 1822-31	
Providence, Rhode Island		1820-44	1820-24, 1828, 1830	
Richmond, Virginia		1866		
Rochester, N. Y.		1829-34	1829	
Sag Harbor, New York		1821-27, 1870	1822-24, 1827	2 Jan. 1916-13 May 1926
St. Andrews, Florida		1865		
St. Augustine, Florida				15 Dec. 1926-1 March 1941
St. Johns, Florida				
St. Petersburg, Florida		1865-66	1823	
Salem and Beverly, Mass.		1820	1820	
Sandusky, Ohio		1820-68	1820-23, 1825-26, 1831	5 June 1906-6 Dec. 1945
Savannah, Georgia		1820		
Saybrook, Connecticut				Nov. 1898-Dec. 1945
Tampa, Florida		1820-33	1820-21	
Waldoboro, Maine		1820-48	1828-29, 1831	
Washington, North Carolina				8 Sept. 1920-21 Nov. 1945
West Palm Beach, Florida		1820-48	1819, 1829	
Wilmington, Del., (see also entry for Delaware)				
Wiscasset, Maine		1820		
Yarmouth, Maine				

[98]

1. A customs district is a geographical area under the jurisdiction of a collector of customs. There may be one or more ports of entry within a district.

2. There are lists of arrivals at Charlestown, Mass., among the copies and abstracts and among the State Department transcripts for Boston. Likewise there are lists of arrivals at Falmouth, Maine, among the copies and abstracts and among the State Department transcripts for Portland.

3. Sometimes shown in the Customs records as the District of South Carolina.

4. The Mayport, Fla., copies of immigration passenger lists include at least one for Jacksonville, Fla., that of 24 February 1916.

5. The National Archives Library has typewritten abstracts of lists of arrivals at New Orleans, 1818-67. The abstracts are in 5 bound volumes (originally 6). The missing volume covered arrivals, 1862 and 1863.

TABLE B

INDEXES TO THE PASSENGER LISTS IN THE NATIONAL ARCHIVES

Name of port or district	Customs passenger lists Card indexes	Immigration passenger lists	
		Card indexes	Book indexes
Baltimore, Maryland	1820-97		
Boston, Massachusetts	1848-91		1 April 1899-14 Sept. 1940
Gulfport, Mississippi	---	1897-July 1952	
Miami, Florida		1902-31 Dec. 1920	
New Bedford, Massachusetts	1875-99	27 Aug. 1904-28 Aug. 1954	
New Orleans, Louisiana	1853-1902	30 Dec. 1929-23 Feb. 1942	
New York, New York	1820-46	1 July 1902-18 Nov. 1954 Oct. 1900-1952	
Pascagoula, Mississippi		16 June 1897-31 Dec. 1943	1 Jan. 1906-31 Dec. 1942
Philadelphia, Pennsylvania	1820-1906 [1]	15 July 1903-21 May 1935	
Portland, Maine	---	1 Jan. 1883-28 June 1948	14 May 1906-17 June 1926
Providence, Rhode Island	---	29 Jan. 1893-22 Nov. 1954	Apr. 1907-6 Apr. 1930
Miscellaneous ports in Alabama, Florida, Georgia, and South Carolina	---	18 June 1911-5 Oct. 1934	13 Dec. 1911-26 June 1934
Miscellaneous ports, not including New York	1820-74	1890-1924	

1. Includes entries for the names of passengers found on cargo manifests, 1800-1819, and later.

Index of Authors and Contributors

NUMBERS refer to items, not pages. The index includes titles of unsigned articles appearing in magazines and of anonymous books.

Adams, Arthur 8
Adams, Nathaniel 31
Adler, Cyrus 1
Alger, Arthur M. 57
"American Passenger Lists, 1804–6" 26
Ames, Azel 33C
Anderson, Rasmus B. 107–107A
Appleton, William S. 48
Armstrong, Edward 119A
Aspinwall, Algernon Aikin 33B

Bailey, Rosalie Fellows 83
Balderston, Marion 120
Banks, Charles Edward 5 34–35 39 53A
Battle, J. H. 117 122
Bellinger, Lyle Frederick 99
Bergen, Van Brunt 84
Blegen, Theodore 107B
Boer, Louis P. de 195
Bolton, Charles Knowles 32
Bolton, Ethel Stanwood 63–63A
Boogher, William Fletcher 225
Boston. Registry Department A Volume of Records Relating to the Early History of Boston Containing Miscellaneous Papers 64
Bowman, William Dodgson 11
Boys, William 46B
Bradford, William 33
Braun, Fritz 139–139B 148–148C 173 247 249–250
Bristol, England Bristol and America 11
Brock, R. A. 224
Brown, Charlotte C. 113B
Browning, Charles H. 123
Brumbaugh, Gaius Marcus 131

Cadbury, Henry J. 254
Calder, Isabel MacBeath 71
Cameron, Viola Root 21
Camp, Anthony J. 10
Campbell, Colin 61
Childs, St Julien R. 233A
Clarke, Louise Brownell 49
Clausen, C. A. 255
Cogwill, E. B. 119B

Colonial Records of Virginia 208–1
"Communication from Governor Francis Nicholson of Virginia Regarding Huguenot Refugees on Board Ship 'Mary and Ann'" 222
Cook, Lewis D. 110B
Cope, Gilbert 124A
Corbit, W. F. 130
Coulter, E. Merton 239–240
Cox, John, Jr 54A
Cramton, Louis C. 252
Curry, Kate Singer 207

Dart, Albert Laplace 242
Dart, Henry P. 242
de Boer, Louis P. 195
"Deutsche Einzeleinwanderer und Familien in Neu-Niederland" 73
Differderffer, Frank Reid 142
Donovan, George Francis 36
Drake, Samuel G. 43A–44B
Dunlap, A. R. 196

Early, Charles Montague 28
"Early Irish Emigrants to America, 1803–1806" 25
"Early Swiss Settlers" 153
Egle, William Henry 145
"Einwanderer in Pennsylvania vor 1700" 116
Ellis, Eilish 258
"Emigrants in the Hercules of Sandwich" 46C
Eno, Joel N. 72
Evjen, John O. 77

Farmer, John 43 68
Faust, Albert Bernhardt 131
Fernow, Berthold 81 85 108
Fields, S. Helen 113
"First Settlers of New Hampshire" 31
Fogg, John S. H. 57
"Foreign Protestants for Carolina in 1679" 233
Forsyth, Hewitt L. 245
Fothergill, Gerald 13 20–20A 23–24

Index of Authors and Contributors, cont'd

France, R. Sharpe *220*
Frank, Karl Friedrich von *260*
Freeman, Wallace R. *103*
French, Elizabeth *14–14A*
Fries, Adelaide L. *231 240–1*
Froehlich, Hugo *158–158A*
Futhey, J. Smith *124A*

Gammon, William J. *230*
Gerber, Adolf *133–135 137*
Gillingham, Harrold E. *157*
Giuseppi, Montague Spencer *19*
Glasgow, William Melancthon *113A*
Goodwin, John A. *34B*
Gookin, Frederick William *214*
Greer, George Cabell *216*

Hackett, J. Dominick *27–27A*
Harding, N. Dermott *11*
Hargreaves-Mawdsley, R. *11*
Hasbrouck, Kenneth E. *87*
Havens, Henry H. *104*
Hiden, Martha Woodroof *210 219*
Hill, Mrs Georgie A. *67*
Hills, Leon Clark *34C 37*
Hinke, William John *146–147 153 179–180*
Hoffman, William J. *16 82*
Hollander, Jacob Harry *18*
Holman, Winifred Lovering *213*
Hotten, John Camden *1*
Hühner, Leon *102*
Hull, William I. *127*

'Immigrants to America before 1750" *2*
Ireland, Gordon *55 199*
Ireland, Northern. Public Record Office *Report of the Deputy Keeper of the Records for the year 1929 26*
Ives, J. Moss *198B*

James, Mrs F. O. *243*
Jamieson, J. Franklin *78B*
Jervey, Theodore D. *235*
Jester, Annie Lash *210*
Jewett, Vivian Holland *229*
Jewson, Charles Boardman *51*
Johnson, Robert G. *110A 111*
Jones, William Macfarlane *221 226*
Jordan, John W. *155 164*

Keen, G. B. *193–194*
Kelker, Luther R. *189*
Kellogg, Lucy Mary *257*
King, Mrs W. W. *228*
Knittle, Walter Allen *90–91A 93 94A 97*
Koehler, Albert F. *112*
Koger, Marvin V. *144*
Krebs, Friedrich *17 132 139–141 150–152 156 159 162–163 167–172 174–178 181–182*
Kuhns, Maude Pinney *41*

Langguth, Otto *136–136A*
Lea, J. Henry *56*
LeFevre, Ralph *87A*
"Lijst van Eenige Koloniers door Kiliaen Van Rensselaer in de Jaren 1636–1642 uit het Vaderland naar Zijne Kolonie Gezonden" *79*
Lilly, Mrs Grant E. *223*
Lindsay, Margaret B. *113B*
"List of Arrivals per 'Pennsylvania Packet,' 1775" *187*
"A List of German Emigrants, 1773" *186*
"List of German Passengers Arrived in the Port, Philadelphia, in the Ship Margaret, from Amsterdam, C. E. Gardner, Master, September 19th, 1804. As Taken from the Original Immigrant List on File in the Division of Public Records, Harrisburg, Pa." *191*
"List of Passengers, 1654 to 1664" *83*
"List of Passengers to America. From Authentic Sources" *33D*
List of Passengers Who Came to Plymouth in The "Mayflower" on Her First Trip in 1620 33F
"List of Servants Who Sailed from Dublin February 25th 1746/7 on the Euryal, and Arrived at Philadelphia April 11th" *166*
"List of the Pilgrims of the 'Welcome'" *119*
"Lists of Germans from the Palatinate Who Came to England in 1709" *91*
"Lists of the Livinge & the Dead in Virginia February 16, 1623" *208–1*
Locke, John G. *38*
Lohr, Otto *116*
Lord, Mary P. *246*
Lorenz, Margaret MacKinnon *11*
"A Lyst of Pasingers Abord the Speedwell of London, Robert Lock Master, Bound for New England" *54*

McCracken, George E. *121*
MacWethy, Lou D. *90A 92 95A 96A 97A 98A–99*
Marshall, William Forbes *11–1*
"Mayflower Descendents and Their Marriages" *33G*
"The Mayflower Series of Papers: 2" *33E*
Middlebrook, Louis F. *160*
"Minutes of the Council and General Court, 1622–1624" *215*
Mörsdorf, Robert *15 244*
Moore, Charles B. *7*
"Moravian Brethren in Heidelberg, 1752" *180*
"Moravian Pioneers in the Swatara Valley, 1752" *179*
Morton, Oren F. *228A*
"Muster of Inhabitants in Virginia. Taken in 1625. Total, 1,095. The Muster of the Inhabitants at Wariscoyack, Taken the 7th of February, 1625" *212*
Myers, Albert Cook *125–126*

"Names and Occupations of Newburgh Palatines" *90B*
"Naturalization of Maryland Settlers in Pennsylvania" *206*
"Naturalizations, Germantown, Pa. 3/7/ 1691/92" *129*
Neible, George W. *165*
Neill, Edward Duffield *198C 201 211*
Nelson, William *109*
Newman, Harry Wright *198A*
Newsome, A. R. *232–232A*
Nicholson, Cregoe D. P. *12*
Nugent, Nell Marion *208*

"The Oath of Abjuration, 1715–1716" *98–1*
O'Brien, Michael J. *66 216A*
O'Callaghan, Edmund Bailey *75–75A 78 86 88 90C 95 96 98 100 197*
Odhner, C. T. *193*

"A Partial List of the Families Who Arrived at Philadelphia between 1682 and 1687. With the Dates of Their Arrival" *124*
"A Partial List of the Families Who Resided in Bucks County, Pennsylvania, Prior to 1687" *117A*
"A Passenger List of Mennonite Immigrants from Russia in 1878" *262*

"Passenger List of Ship 'Catherine'" *259*
"Passenger List of the Ship 'Elizabeth' Which Arrived at Philadelphia in 1819" *192*
"Passenger Lists 1657 to 1664" *86A*
[Passenger manifest of the ship *Atlantic*, 1834] *251*
[Passenger manifest of the ship *Manhattan*, 1820] *106*
"Passengers for New England" *59 62*
"Passengers from the Rhineland to Pennsylvania" *149*
"Passengers of the Mary and John, 1634" *45*
"Passengers to America" *57*
Patten, Jennie M. *101*
Pennsylvania (Colony). Provincial Council *Minutes of the Provincial Council of Pennsylvania from the Organization to the Termination of the Proprietary Government* *138–138A*
Perez, L. *242–1*
Perry, William Stevens *226A*
"Persons Naturalized in the Province of Pennsylvania" *161*
Potter, Elisha R. *69*
Prindle, Paul W. *17–1*
Putnam, Eben *46*

Raskob, John Jacob *198*
Raven, John J. *253*
Ravenel, Daniel *234*
"Record of Indentures of Individuals Bound Out as Apprentices, Servants, Etc. and of German and Other Redemptioners in the Office of the Mayor of the City of Philadelphia, October 3, 1771, to October 5, 1773" *184*
Redstone, Vincent B. *9*
Revill, Janie *238*
Richardson, Hester Dorsey *198D 202A 203A*
Rider, Sidney S. *70*
Ritz, Albrecht *16–1 19–1*
Roberts, Charles R. *143*
Rogers, Albert R. *40*
"The Roll off Those Who Haue Taken the Oath of Allegiance in the Kings County in the Province of New Yorke the 26: 27: 28: 29: and 30 Day off September in the Third Yeare of His May[tsh] Raigne Annoq[ue] Domine 1687" *88A*
Rupp, Daniel Israel *144*

Index of Authors and Contributors, cont'd

"The Sailing of the Ship 'Submission' in the Year 1682, with a True Copy of the Vessel's Log" *118*

Savage, James *46B 47*

Saye, Albert B. *240*

Scharf, J. Thomas *198E 200 202 203 205*

Scheben, Joseph *256*

Schermerhorn, Richard, Jr *74*

Schermerhorn, William E. *111A*

"Scotch Prisoners Sent to Massachusetts in 1652, by Order of the English Government" *53*

Scott, William Wallace *227*

Seacord, Morgan H. *89*

Sherwood, George *4*

"Ship Lists of Passengers Leaving France for Louisiana, 1718–1724" *242*

Shurtleff, Nathaniel Bradstreet *33A*

Sickler, Joseph S. *110*

Simmendinger, Ulrich *94*

Smith, Ervin Peter, Sr *245*

Smith, Henry A. M. *236*

Smith, R. G. *183*

Smith, Samuel *111*

Somerby, H. G. *217*

Spain. Archivo General de Indias, Seville *Catálogo de Pasajeros a Indias durante los Siglos XVI, XVII y XVIII 241*

Spencer, Wilbur D. *30*

Spengemann, Friedrich *248*

Stanard, William Glover *218*

Stapleton, Ammon *128*

Steinemann, Ernst *154*

Stevens, Henry *52*

Stevenson, John R. *115*

Stewart, Robert Armistead *208*

The Story of Sloanes 251

Strassburger, Ralph Beaver *146*

Thwing, Annie Haven *50*

"Time of the Arrival in New England of the Following Ministers" *42*

Tyler, Lyon Gardiner *209*

United States. State Department *Letter from the Secretary of State, with a Transcript of the List of Passengers Who Arrived in the United States from the 1st October, 1819, to the 30th September, 1820 29*

United States. Work Projects Administration *Index to Records of Aliens' Declarations of Intention and/or Oaths of Allegiance, 1789–1880 188*

Van Laer, Arnold Johan Ferdinand *76 80*

"Van Tienhoven's Answer to the Vertoogh" *78A*

"Various Sailings from Scotland to Boston between 1716 and 1766" *65*

Virkus, Frederick A. *3*

Voigt, Gilbert P. *237*

Walterscheid, J. *261*

Waters, Henry F. *57–58 60–60A*

Weber, Ludwig *153*

Wells, Frederic Palmer *102–1*

White, Frank F., Jr *204*

Whitehead, William A. *113C*

Wodrow, Robert *114*

Wolfe, Richard J. *102 105*

Yoder, Don *22 135–136 151 154 158 172 190*

Index of Ship Names

THIS is an analytical index to the sources listed in the preceding bibliography. An example will suffice to show how the entries have been made. After *Belinda* the numerals *165*(32:92–96) stand for volume 32, pages 92–96 of item *165* in the bibliography (which is George W. Neible's "Servants and Apprentices Bound and Assigned before James Hamilton Mayor of Philadelphia 1745," printed in volumes 30–32 of *The Pennsylvania Magazine of History and Biography*).

Names spelled in several different ways but similar phonetically, as Abigail, also spelled Abigal, Abbigal, Abigale, are entered under the accepted modern spelling. Authorities used were J. B. Lippincott's *Gazetteer*, 1893, for place names and Flora H. Loughhead's *Dictionary of Given Names*, 1934, for personal names.

A

Abaellino *29*(247)

Abeona *29*(16)

Abigail *1*(73, 87, 92, 96–100, 201, 206, 209, 212, 215, 220–224, 227, 229, 231, 233, 238, 240–242, 248, 253, 256, 258–262); (108); *2*(9, 17, 35, 40, 76–77, 79–80, 133, 154, 207–208); *5*(1, 6, 12, 19, 32, 36–37, 48, 52, 99, 108, 113, 168–169, 171); *7*(73); *8*(38); *11*(182); *29*(55, 142, 229, 242); *30* (150); *35*(59, 161); *36*(36, 40); *44* (28, 31–33, 35–38); *44A*(313–320); *47*(8:262, 264–269); *64*(245, 249, 251, 260, 266, 280, 284, 301, 316); *210* (5, 11, 14, 17, 20, 25–29, 32, 34, 36, 39, 43–47, 53, 58, 61–63, 64–66); *211* (73–74); *212*(217–218)

Abraham *1*(138); *2*(28, 41, 71); *30* (19); *217*(15:146)

Abraham & Francis *12*(12:381, 404–406, 441–442, 479; 13:48, 78–79)

Abraham & Isaac *11*(164, 168)

Abraham & Mary *11*(174–175)

Acolus *145*(645)

Active *20*(114, 116); *20A*(64:314, 316); *24*(60:346); *28*(206); *29*(18, 87, 99)

Actress *28*(206); *29*(16)

Adallio *29*(256)

Addam *1*(241); *2*(212); *210*(46); *212* (217)

Adela *29*(239)

l'Adele *29*(41, 98)

Adeline *29*(32, 41, 179, 219)

Admiral Hawk *238*(97)

Adolph *146*(3:3, 5)

Adriana *29*(94)

Adventure *1*(362); *2*(28, 44, 210); *11* (145, 173); *12*(12:193, 379; 13:49, 79); *20*(69–70, 88, 137, 151–152); *20A*(63:343–344; 64:24; 65:30, 125–126); *21*(35); *29*(28); *63*(114); *63A* (65:540); *64*(229, 231, 239, 241); *138* (3:305, 486); *138A*(3:288, 455); *144* (326); *145*(430); *146* Galley (1:14); *151*(6:Spring 1955, 38)

Adventure Galley *146*(1:15, 83, 85–86, 600–601, 603–604)

Adventurer *2*(10, 80, 195); *20*(68, 123–124); *20A*(63:342; 64:323–324); *63* (115); *63A*(65:541); *143*(7, 12); *144* (53, 78); *145*(10, 57)

Advice *64*(249)

Adze *29*(273)

Aegir *254*(39)

Aeolus *27*(82); *27A*(June 1929:12; Dec 1926:31); *28*(206); *29*(67); *146*(3: 181–182)

Africa *27*(82); *27A*(June 1926:10–11)

l'African *29*(109)

Agawam *29*(138)

Agnes *29*(84, 114); *185*(33:475)

Agreement *11*(94, 137–139, 143–144, 160–161, 165, 167–168); *199*(73)

Agricola *29*(287)

Ajax *21*(72); *29*(203); *232*(13); *232A* (51)

Akin Alexander *27A*(Dec 1926:23)

Index of Ship Names, continued

Alabama 29(24)
Albany 2(10); 135(157–158); 138(3: 347); 138A(3:329); 144(56, 193); 145(14, 280); 146(1:20–21, 394); 151 (6:Spring 1955, 37)
Albert 29(57, 74, 144, 205, 217, 221)
Albion 20(45–46, 48, 50); 20A(63:135–136, 138, 140); 29(9, 109–110)
Aleine 29(51)
Alert 29(146, 175, 213)
Alexander 1(73); 2(151, 182, 207); 4 (ser 1:72); 11(160); 27(82); 27A (Dec 1926:32); 29(26, 33, 37, 42, 98, 179, 182, 224, 239, 242); 44(105); 44A(352); 63(13); 63A(63:189); 185 (33:475)
Alexander & Ann 138(3:410); 138A(3: 386); 144(64); 145(21); 146(1:34–35)
Alexander Ann 2(92)
Alexander Mansfield 29(137–138)
Alexandria 22(82); 29(227); 243(27)
Alexis 24(61:269)
Alfred 29(235)
Algernon 27(82); 27A(June 1926:5–6
Alice 1(109); 2(17, 91); 8(38); 217(5: 61)
Alithea 11(162, 164, 167, 174); 199(73) *See also* Althea.
Allen 2(52); 63(20); 63A(63:272); 64 (233); 138(3:391); 138A(3:368); 144 (60); 145(18); 146(1:27, 29–30)
Alligator 29(262)
Almira 29(61)
Alonzo 29(139, 227)
Alpha 28(206); 29(138)
Alpha & Omega 29(55)
Althea 11(157–158) *See also* Alithea.
Amazon 29(21, 157–158, 180, 283); 64 (292)
Ambrose 1(256); 35(65); 39(33–34); 210(61)
Ambuscade 29(15, 271)
Amelia 20(12, 89); 20A(62:250; 64: 106); 29(125)
America 1(95); 2(85, 101, 103, 127, 164); 11(175–176); 20(94); 20A(64: 110); 29(53, 257); 36(36, 40); 64 262, 264, 266, 268, 277, 281, 283, 287, 292, 294, 299, 302, 305, 310, 313–314, 317); 124(339); 124A(24); 144(394); 145(495, 556, 567, 575); 146(1:733; 3:49, 82, 90, 96); 189(194); 217(3: 388)

American 24(60:161; 61:135, 268)
American Merchant 2(19); 11(159, 162, 165, 173, 175–176); 201(202)
Amherst 20(57); 20A(63:234); 63(24); 63A(63:276); 64(290, 303)
Amiable Creole 145(578); 146(3:100)
Amiable Matilda 145(559); 146(3:100)
Amity 1(134); 2(171); 11(169, 173); 29(129–130, 249); 44(111); 44A (356); 63(28, 104, 219); 63A(63:280; 65:128; 67:323); 64(232); 65(14); 117(676); 117A(231); 124(340); 124A(24)
Amphion 28(205); 29(90)
Amsterdam Packet 145(532); 146(3:34)
Anderson 2(12, 114); 135(142, 153, 163, 169, 182, 202–204, 231); 144(232, 246, 280); 145(315, 328, 359); 146 (1:435, 450, 488); 151(7:Spring 1956, 39); 154(189, 195); 171(31); 174(9)
Andes 29(245)
Andrew Jackson 29(13, 104)
Andromache 29(10, 58); 67(208)
Angel Gabriel 2(59, 122); 5(5, 87); 11 (165–166); 30(112); 35(160); 199 (73)
Angelina 29(29)
l'Angle 29(39)
Ann 1(xxix, 211, 230–231, 239, 246–247, 249, 255, 262); 2(51–52, 95, 129); 20(60, 126, 138); 20A(63:237; 64:326; 65:31–32); 27(82); 29(9, 28–29, 88, 159); 36(1, 36); 44B(121); 63(212); 63A(67:316); 64(239, 248, 258–259, 296, 307, 310); 135(146, 149–150, 170, 184–185, 189, 202, 214, 217, 237); 144(173–174, 214, 278); 145(254, 298, 357, 579); 146(1:359, 361, 416); 146(1:486); 147(108); 210(15, 35–36, 44, 51–52, 54, 59, 66); 215(131)
Ann & Elizabeth 1(70); 2(115, 172, 175, 182, 184); 44(104); 44A(351–352); 117(680); 117A(233)
Ann & Jane 2(187)
Ann & Margaret 36(38); 64(297); 66 (186)
Ann & Mary 14A(64:258); 14(17)
Ann & Sarah 14(4, 13, 15, 32); 14A(64: 159, 254, 256; 65:43)
Ann Maria 29(13, 285)
Ann Penney 64(305)
Ann Rowland 29(285)
Anna 57(30:42); 64(229, 234, 239); 146(3:106, 108)

Anna & Mary 64(242)

Anna Maria 11(182); 29(13); 243(28)

Annabelle 65(15)

Anne 2(149); 4(ser 1:11); 5(12–13, 17, 20, 43, 50, 85, 100, 103, 111, 113, 123, 132–133, 167); 11(181); 28(205); 34 (133–165, 175–178); 34A(35); 34B (242–244, 297–300); 34C(84–86); 34D(2); 35(52); 165(30:350, 427, 432–433; 31:86, 89); 239

Anne & Mary 12(12:270–272, 307, 341, 519, 552)

Anne & Rebecca 63(71); 63A(64:271)

Anne & Susa 4(ser 1:32)

Annes 30(205)

Annthea Bell 29(86)

Anntie 2(163)

Anson 29(141, 219)

Antelope 2(81, 90, 91); 29(97, 195, 257); 117(672); 117A(224); 124(329); 124A (22); 145(628); 146(3:161–162)

Antigua Merchant 11(168–169)

Anton 29(26)

Antony 29(5)

Apnes 29(240)

Apollo 63(206); 63A(67:310); 64(292); 145(542); 146(3:67)

Apprentice 64(274)

Arab 29(225)

Arabella 2(81, 86, 101); 5(45, 52, 157); 35(65); 39(25, 30, 35–37, 41, 43–44, 108); 40(15, 17); 43(137, 139); 44 (78); 59(407)

Archangel 30(14)

Archer 29(217)

Ardent 24(60:163)

de Arent. See Eagle.

Aretas 29(182)

Aristides 29(215, 227)

Aristo 29(125)

Aristobulus 29(224)

Ark 2(27, 38, 58, 84, 161); 4(ser 1:23); 198(95); 198A–198E

Armes of Bristol 11(138–139)

Arms of Norway 75(438); 75A(135) See also het Wapen van Noorwegen.

Armunda 29(180)

Arnold 20(61); 20A(63:237)

Arrethia 29(179)

Arthur & Mary 11(166, 169, 172)

Arthurian 29(39)

Ashton Hall 20(155–156); 20A(65:129)

Asia 29(180)

Assistance 12(12:481–482, 516; 13:107–108, 145–148, 175–176, 179)

Assurance 1(110); 2(27, 31, 46, 49, 57, 77, 101, 107, 125, 127, 129, 131, 134, 142, 160, 165, 173, 212); 217(5:61)

Astrea 29(229)

Athenian 29(34, 231); 243(27)

Athens 29(161–162)

Atlanta 27A(June 1926:18–19); 29(34–35)

Atlantic 24(66:306); 29(87, 105–106, 115–116, 255); 145(649, 655); 146(3: 149, 153, 189, 191); 251

Atrevida 29(268)

Atticus 29(143)

Augustine 14(43); 14A(65:169)

Auntie. See Anntie.

Aurora 2(56, 98, 129); 29(125, 151); 135(215); 144(168); 145(250); 146 (1:352–353)

Ayres 29(180)

Azariah 29(24, 153–154)

Azuba 64(257)

B

Bacchus 145(566); 146(3:89)

Bachelor 1(118); 2(132); 5(31); 21(6); 44(41); 44A(322); 232(17, 25); 232A (130, 138) See also Batchellor.

Bachelors Delight 1(357)

Bahama 64(232)

Baily 4(ser 1:57)

Bainbridge 29(206)

Balize 29(48)

Balloon 29(21, 180)

Baltic 29(180)

Baltimore 11(143, 159); 12(12:123, 159); 20(61–62, 125, 161–162); 20A 63:237–239; 64:325; 65:233–234); 64 (245, 250)

Baltimore Packet 20(136); 20A(65:29)

Bannister 2(204); 135(206–207, 225, 236); 144(340); 145(443); 146(1: 645–648); 151(8:Summer 1956, 58)

Baraco 243(28)

Barbados Merchant 1(355, 370, 408); 2 (200); 11(143–144); 12(12:230–232, 516–517); 14(16); 14A(64:257)

Barbara 67(207)

Barbary 29(145)

Barclay 28(206); 29(41); 135(159, 196, 203, 220–221); 144(324); 145(429); 146(1:595, 597–598, 600); 151(7: Winter 1956, 38, Spring 1956, 39) 175 (177–178)

Barnaby 12(12:160–161, 194)

Index of Ship Names, continued

Barsheba *64*(315)
Batchellor *2*(132); *7*(76); *11*(160–163, 165–166, 176); *35*(153); *47*(8:271); *64*(314) See also Bachelor.
Bawley *144*(290); *145*(368)
Beanguaze *29*(237)
Bear *2*(203); *83*(5); *84*(181)
Beaufort *20*(116, 170); *20A*(64:316; 65: 242)
Beaver *2*(7, 61); *29*(92); *35*(202); *64* (277); *83*(5, 10, 17, 27); *84*(181–182); *86*(35, 37, 42); *86A*(144, 150, 158) See also de Bever.
Bee *29*(99, 205); *243*(27)
de Beer. *See* Bear.
Beginning *1*(365, 387, 393, 404, 414); *64*(231)
Beith *20*(92); *20A*(64:108)
Belfast *29*(17, 241)
Belfast Packet *238*(64)
Belinda *165*(32:92–96, 98–99, 237)
Belisarius *27*(82); *27A*(June 1926:14–15); *29*(5, 145); *67*(208); *144*(375–376)
Bellar *20*(53); *20A*(63:142)
Belle *29*(131)
Belle Savage *29*(262)
Beluga *29*(58)
Belvidere *29*(24, 103, 169, 199); *145* (583); *146*(3:112, 114)
Benedict Father *12*(12:379)
Benedict Leonard *12*(12:343–344, 381–382, 404–405; 13:47–50, 80)
Benjamin *11*(169); *29*(71); *55*(388); *56* (334); *64*(316)
Bennett Galley *2*(11–12, 135); *144* (225); *145*(309); *146*(1:428); *175* (181)
Betsey *2*(13, 113, 131, 160); *20*(40, 94, 142–143); *20A*(63:27–28; 64:110; 65: 116); *24*(61:136); *29*(104, 191–192, 230, 250); *36*(34, 39); *64*(245, 247, 254, 263–264, 266–267, 278–279, 287, 290–291, 295, 301, 303–305, 307–309, 313, 315, 317); *135*(155, 214, 221); *139*(39, 42); *139A*(5:31; 6:40); *139B* (7, 16); *141*(245); *144*(133–134, 371, 374, 386, 398); *145*(188, 473, 476, 487, 499, 659); *146*(1:257–258, 260–262, 706, 710, 723, 738; 3:12, 194); *151*(6:Winter 1954–55, 39, Spring 1955, 37; 8:Summer 1956, 58); *152* (63); *175*(180); *185*(33:475)

Betsey & John *36*(40); *64*(311)
Betsey & Ruth *64*(258)
Betsy Rutledge *189*(194)
Betty *1*(320, 320*, 322, 325); *20*(52); *20A*(63:142); *64*(238, 281)
Betty Grett. *See* Gregg.
Beulah *20*(118); *20A*(64:318); *135* (159, 191); *136*(228); *144*(299); *145* (380); *146*(1:512–513, 515–516); *151* (8:Summer 1956, 58)
de Bever *77*(184, 421). *See also* Beaver.
Beverly *29*(225)
Bevis *1*(298); *2*(27, 45, 99, 122, 153, 217, 219); *5*(60, 62, 64, 180); *30* (150); *35*(198); *44*(60–61); *44A* (336–337); *47*(10:144, 146)
Bideford *64*(284, 288, 311)
Big Brothers *29*(168)
Bilboa *64*(291)
Bingham *29*(67)
Bird *35*(106)
Birmingham Packet *145*(548); *146*(3: 72)
Black Prince *20*(168); *20A*(65:240)
Blackburn *64*(283)
Blackmore (139, 159–160, 163–164, 166-167)
Bland *20*(147–148); *20A*(65:120)
Blessing *1*(93, 108, 206, 223–224, 351, 357–358, 362, 368, 388); *2*(10, 173); *4*(ser 1:15; ser 2:109); *5*(43, 50, 58, 78); *7*(75); *30*(17); *35*(176); *44*(34, 40); *44A*(317, 321); *47*(8:267, 270); *63*(99); *63A*(65:123); *208*(xxix); *210* (11, 28–29, 45)
Bliederman *145*(583); *146*(3:111)
Blizzard *64*(270)
Blooming Rose *29*(111)
Bold Adventure *1*(298)
Bolodore *243*(25)
Bolton *165*(30:350–352, 427–429, 431; 31:83–84, 91)
Bona Nova *1*(201–202, 213–215, 217, 220, 223–224, 226, 230–236, 239, 244–245, 249–250, 252–264); *2*(17, 19, 184, 189); *30*(19); *210*(5–6, 18–20, 22, 25, 27, 29–30, 35–36, 38–41, 43, 49–50, 54–55, 57–61, 63–68); *211*(71)
Bonaventura *1*(35, 202, 205, 224, 229, 233, 264); *2*(7–9, 31, 54–55, 83, 90, 98, 147); *210*(6, 10, 29, 35, 38); *217* (2:112)
Bonaventure Deal *2*(179)
Bonny Bess *2*(216); *210*(7, 30, 42–43, 45, 49, 51); *215*(133)

Bonny Bessie *1*(202, 225, 227, 237–238, 240, 244, 246)

de Bonte Koe *2*(21, 72); *77*(139, 247, 254, 268, 282, 312, 403, 407, 413, 417, 424, 431, 433); *112*(3, 23) *See also* Spotted Cow.

Booer *29*(13)

Booth *12*(12:306, 308–309, 340, 342–343, 379–380, 406, 440; 13:12–13, 47, 49); *63*(189); *63A*(67:213)

Bordeaux *29*(105)

Boscowan *36*(35); *64*(250, 256, 276, 305, 316)

Boston *29*(241–242); *144*(367); *145* (469); *146*(1:702); *172*(9)

Boston Merchant *11*(182); *55*(388); *63* (23); *63A*(63:275); *64*(233)

Boston Packet *20*(57, 75); *20A*(63:234, 349); *64*(256, 265, 278, 291, 305, 312); *145*(577); *146*(3:99–100)

Boudain *28*(206)

Bounty *2*(71)

Bourbon *243*(25)

Braddock *29*(231)

Brandt *29*(61, 198)

de Brant van Trogen *77*(156, 193, 237, 359) *See also* Fire of Troy.

le Brie *146*(3:30)

Brig *36*(35)

Bright Phoebus *29*(105)

Brilliant *20*(53–54); *20A*(63:142, 144)

Brisk *29*(38)

Bristol *28*(206); *64*(252, 262); *145* (526); *146*(3:22)

Bristol Comfort *124*(333); *124A*(23)

Bristol Factor *2*(210); *11*(166, 169–170, 172); *177*(673); *117A*(225)

Bristol Merchant *2*(8, 147); *11*(160–161, 163–167, 171, 173, 181); *117*(672); *117A*(224); *124*(336); *124A*(23); *199* (73)

Bristoll Armes. *See* Armes of Bristol.

Britannia *2*(21, 25, 47, 90, 121, 189, 203); *14*(37); *14A*(65:49); *20*(114, 133); *20A*(64:314; 65:26); *29*(18); *64*(236, 246, 267, 275, 282, 284, 295, 297–298, 302, 304, 308); *135*(208); *138*(3:441); *138A*(3:414); *139*(41); *139A*(6:39); *139B*(15); *142*(212); *143*(10); *144*(67–68, 359, 380, 392, 408); *145*(28, 462, 482, 493, 508); *146*(1:47, 51, 53, 692, 717, 730, 749); *151*(7:Winter 1956, 39; 8:Summer 1956, 57); *173*(13); *182*(12); *185*

(33:475–476); *186*(113); *238*(62, 83, 128)

British Liberality *243*(27)

Briton *20*(73, 117); *20A*(63:347, 64: 317); *67*(209); *232*(5, 9); *232A*(43, 47)

Broken Heart *77*(360); *84*(182); *86* (42) *86A*(158)

Brotherhood *2*(26, 208); *135*(199); *144* (243); *145*(325); *146*(1:447); *151* (6:Spring 1955, 38); *174*(9)

Brothers *2*(99, 195, 203); *20*(73–74); *20A*(63:347–348); *24*(61:347); *29* (105, 266); *135*(132, 167, 188, 191, 198, 207); *136*(220); *139*(41); *139A* (5:36); *139B*(13); *141*(240); *144* (233, 257, 274, 311, 328); *145*(316, 338, 353, 402, 432, 541, 548); *146*(1: 436, 463, 481, 550, 552–553, 609–613; 3:60, 71); *151*(7:Spring 1956, 39); *169*(13); *171*(31)

Brothers Adventure *1*(384, 401, 405); *12* (12:305, 308, 342; 13:11–12)

Brothers Society *64*(234, 241)

Brownfish *2*(21); *83*(7); *84*(181); *86* (33); *86A*(142) *See also* de Bruyn-vis.

Brutus *25*(22); *29*(39, 90, 237); *64*(280)

de Bruynvis *2*(11); *77*(55, 272, 428) *See also* Brownfish.

Buffalo *29*(9, 18, 85, 227, 247)

Burnaby. *See* Barnaby.

Burnham *64*(289)

Bute *64*(305)

C

Cadmus *29*(37–38)

Caesar *20*(44, 93); *20A*(63:134; 64: 110); *185*(33:475)

Calcutta *29*(213)

Cale *64*(280)

Caledonia *29*(122, 194, 261)

Calieta *2*(121)

den Calmar Sleutel *76*(817); *77*(21) *See also* Key of Calmar.

Calvert *20*(144); *20A*(65:117–118)

Calypso *29*(47)

Camden *20*(156); *20A*(65:129)

Cameron *29*(247)

Camillus *29*(102)

Canada *29*(24, 179)

Candide *145*(523); *146*(1:15–16)

Canton *145*(604); *146*(3:130–131)

Caridao *243*(25)

Index of Ship Names, continued

Carlen 29(99)

Carolina 4(ser 2:200); 20(8, 18, 85, 118, 120); 20A(62:246, 332; 64:21, 319–320); 29(26, 226); 144(406); 145(506, 607); 146(1:747; 3:138); 165(30:350, 431–432); 185(33:475); 232(3, 6); 232A(41, 44); 243(24)

Carolina Packet 20(92); 20A(64:108); 232(6–7, 16); 232A(44–45, 129)

Caroline 29(48, 92)

Carrier 29(96, 253)

Carteret 2(65, 73); 144(172); 145(253); 146(1:357)

Cashier 29(88)

Caspian 29(52)

Castine Packet 29(142)

Castle 5(74, 85); 35(191)

Catherine 2(45, 210); 20(110, 113); 20A (64:224, 227); 24(66:30); 29(29–30, 35–36, 41, 60, 93, 96, 111, 217, 221, 226, 241, 271); 36(39); 56(333); 63 (52, 101); 63A(64:28; 65:125); 64 (247, 307); 66(180); 135(216); 144 (113, 152, 402, 405, 409, 418); 145 (146, 227, 502, 505, 509, 518); 146 (1:197–198, 320–321, 742, 746, 751, 762; 3:49, 51); 155(230, 233); 164(1: 167); 165(31:90, 470); 185(33:476); 243(28); 259

Catherine & Eliza 29(147–148)

Cato 20(79–80); 20A(63:353–354); 64 (279); 145(627); 146(3:160)

Cecilia 64(280); 243(23–25)

Celeste 243(26)

Ceres 24(62:170); 28(206); 29(19, 39, 85–87, 95, 143, 212)

Chalkley 20(127); 20A(65:20)

Champion 29(252)

Chance 2(190); 20(13–14); 20A(62: 251–252); 21(87); 132(11, 18–19, 22–24); 135(142, 168, 213); 136(213, 218); 141(245); 144(350–351, 353, 355, 370, 373); 145(454, 456, 458, 472, 475); 146(1:682, 685, 688, 705, 708); 151(6:Winter 1954–55, 39, Spring 1955, 38); 152(63); 158(46); 158A(61); 159(22–24)

Channing 258(339–347)

Charitas 193(464)

Charity 1(202, 221, 230, 237, 252); 5 (106, 137); 11(166); 29(53–54); 30 (19, 21); 35(57); 210(6, 26, 35, 42, 57); 211(73)

Charles 1(209–210, 231, 233, 240, 249, 253, 264); 2(85); 4(ser 2:150); 11 (92, 162); 12(12:162, 194); 29(219); 30(55); 35(65, 97, 203); 39(33, 45); 117(674); 117A(229); 124(337); 124A(23); 208(xxxiii); 210(14–15, 37–38, 45, 53, 68)

Charles & Harriot 24(61:267)

Charles & Henry 29(227)

Charles Fawcett 28(205–206)

Charles K. Mallory 29(57, 228)

Charleston Packet 29(31)

Charlotta 146(1:339); 147(123)

Charlotte 2(24, 26, 210); 20(34); 20A 63:21); 29(92, 248); 63(150); 63A 66:534); 144(161); 145(239, 596); 146(3:125–127); 185(33:475)

Charlotte Corday 29(8, 13, 102, 125, 272)

Charlotte Laurence 29(67)

Charming Betsey 2(52); 144(93); 145 (98)

Charming Betty 138(3:564); 138A(3: 524); 146(1:134–136)

Charming Hannah 64(272, 275, 277, 281, 296, 300)

Charming Molly 2(210); 20(90); 20A (64:106); 36(33–34); 64(254–255, 257, 264–265, 274, 277, 304, 306, 315); 144(412, 415); 145(512, 515); 146(1:754, 758)

Charming Nancy 2(9, 11, 26, 64, 135, 168); 20(95); 20A(64:111–112); 36 (33); 64(254); 143(19); 144(129); 145(141, 178); 146(1:188, 191–192, 245–247); 151(7:Spring 1956, 39)

Charming Peggy 64(295)

Charming Polly 64(297); 144(110–111)

Charming Sally 64(245, 263, 288)

Chase 29(24, 121, 248)

Chatsworth 29(86)

Chauncy 29(7, 15, 287)

Cherub 29(53, 145, 149–150, 213, 216–217, 219–220, 223)

Chester 165(32:99–103, 237–240, 244, 248, 352, 354, 357)

Chesterfield 2(40); 135(162–163, 175, 177, 189, 191–192, 200, 209, 212, 219, 222, 235); 144(192); 145(279); 146 (1:393); 169(13)

Chichester 238(93)

Christian 1(42); 2(11, 26, 47, 67, 114, 207); 7(71); 35(129, 139); 44(14); 44A(302); 135(232); 144(197–198); 145(284); 146(1:399); 147(108)

Christopher 28(205); 29(191, 225); 47
  (8:252)
Christy 21(61, 87)
Chudley 30(19)
Cicero 64(280)
Cincinnatus 29(123–124)
Circe 29(245)
City of Cork 165(31:89–92, 94–98, 100–
  101, 196)
Clara 29(155)
Clarissa 29(105)
Clarissa Ann 243(27)
Classon 258(340)
Clement & Job 35(108); 44(69)
Clementina 21(81, 85); 144(414); 145
  (514); 146(1:757)
Cleveland 29(70); 165(30:352, 427,
  431, 436; 31:85–86)
Climax 29(56, 146)
Clio 29(89, 145)
Clothier 29(131, 183)
Collector 29(81)
Colonel G. Armistead 29(21, 88)
Colonel Ramsay 29(87)
Columbia 29(28–29, 103, 148, 195, 288);
  145(537, 539, 544, 560, 574, 577); 146
  (3:52, 57–58, 60, 69–70, 94, 98–100);
  189(337)
Columbus 29(180); 243(28); 258(372–
  379)
Combine 29(99)
Comet 29(29, 32, 95, 139, 225–226,
  257); 243(28)
Comfort 11(164–165, 171–172, 174,
  181); 124(333); 124A(23); 199(73)
Commerce 21(1–5, 77); 24(61:351); 29
  (20, 38, 125, 141, 227); 64(271, 280,
  293); 103(136); 145(532, 602); 146
  (3:33, 131, 135)
Commodore Patterson 29(42)
Commodore Perry 29(78)
Commodore Porter 29(189)
Commodore Preble 29(57)
Conception 243(23)
Concord 1(246); 11(94, 145, 166); 14
  (12, 24); 14A(64:252, 338); 20(99);
  20A(64:115); 29(73, 220); 30(13);
  64(233, 292, 305); 83(28); 84(182);
  86(42); 86A(158); 117(673–674,
  679); 117A(228–229); 117(677);
  117A(232); 145(550, 566); 146(3:
  74–75, 89); 210(51) See also de
  Eendracht.
Confiance 29(94)

Confidence 5(5–6, 30, 34, 53, 61–64,
  134, 177–179, 182); 35(195); 44(57,
  60); 44A(334, 336); 52(108)
Congress 29(24)
de Coninck David 2(25); 76(825); 77
  (31, 430)
de Coninck Salmon 77(359)
Conistoga 28(206); 29(64)
Connecticut 29(27)
Connoly 185(33:475)
Conqueror 11(180)
Consent 30(22–23)
Constance 1(136); 2(31, 60, 82, 90, 93,
  205); 9(141, 143); 217(15:145)
Constant Martha 11(158–159); 199(73)
Constant Warwick 2(203)
Constantine 63(158); 63A(67:94)
Constitution 29(228)
Content 11(136, 182); 12(12:90–92);
  29(254); 55(388)
Copernican 29(55)
Cora 29(239)
Cordelia 29(13, 249); 145(653); 146(3:
  187, 189)
Cornelia 24(60:160)
Cossack 29(268)
Couli Can 165(31:90–97, 198, 352, 461)
Count de Toulouse 242(14:517)
Countess of Bute 64(381)
Countess of Dumfries 21(52)
Countess of Sussex 144(373); 145(474);
  146(1:708)
Courier 28(205); 29(14, 273)
Crawford 2(209); 135(188); 141(246);
  144(385, 389, 393, 398, 400, 412); 145
  (486, 490, 494, 499, 501, 512); 146
  (1:722, 728, 732, 737, 740, 755); 151
  (6:Spring 1955, 37; 7:Winter 1956,
  39; 8:Summer 1956, 58); 152(64);
  182(12)
Creole 243(23, 25–26); 258(339–347)
Criterion 29(112, 114)
Crown 2(51); 12(12:233, 269, 517); 64
  (234); 135(236); 144(190); 145
  (277); 146(1:391)
Crown Melago 12(12:405, 480–482)
Cullodian 145(477); 146(1:711)
Culvert 20(143); 20A(65:116)
Curling 232(7–8); 232A(45–46)
Cygnet 29(242); 243(28)
Cynthia 64(313)

D

Dancy 29(179)
Dandy 29(24)

Index of Ship Names, continued

Daniel *11*(163); *64*(240)
Daniel & Elizabeth *117*(678); *117A* (226)
Daniel & James *29*(261–262)
Dart *29*(21, 38)
Dartmouth *64*(279)
Dauphine *243*(26)
David *2*(47, 115, 157, 173, 187); *30* (17), *217*(15:145)
David l'Hommedieu *145*(578); *146*(3: 106)
Davy *2*(10, 100); *132*(20, 24); *144* (125); *145*(169); *146*(1:233, 235); *147*(109)
Deborah *64*(249, 253, 262, 270–271, 286, 300, 313)
Decatur *29*(16, 26, 194–195, 228)
Deep Bay *64*(261, 309–310)
Defence *1*(89–91, 98–101, 105–106); *2* (14); *5*(1, 6, 12, 15, 44, 52, 54, 61, 108); *7*(74); *8*(38); *35*(167); *44* (32, 36–39); *44A*(315–316, 318–320); *47*(8:265–266, 268–269)
Defiance *36*(40); *64*(246, 258, 265, 268, 300, 302, 310, 312, 316)
Delaware *1*(229); *124*(339); *124A*(24); *145*(581); *146*(3:109); *165*(31:467–473; 32:88–91, 95, 98, 100–101); *210* (34); *211*(72)
Delegate *29*(91)
Delight *11*(71); *64*(291)
Deliverance *1*(208, 222, 253); *30*(13); *208*(xxviii–xxix); *210*(13, 27, 57)
Dell Carmen *243*(24)
Demerra *63*(90); *63A*(65:114)
Desire *35*(130, 204); *36*(32, 37); *44* (31, 33, 63); *44A*(315–316, 338); *64* (246, 249, 252–253, 259, 272, 288–289, 300, 303, 306); *124*(338); *124A*(24)
la De Spenser *20*(20); *20A*(62:324)
Deus Soeurs *29*(52)
Devonshire *64*(245, 256, 271, 279, 299)
Devotion *145*(589); *146*(3:117)
Diamond *20*(62); *20 A*(63:239); *64* (270, 314)
Diana *1*(219–220, 231, 234, 237–238, 244, 250, 253, 259, 264); *20*(61–62, 128); *20A*(63:238–239; 65:21–22); *21*(45); *24*(60:347); *29*(121, 247, 276); *64*(246, 278, 298, 304); *145* (580); *146*(3:42, 44, 108–109); *189* (188); *210*(21, 24, 36, 39, 42, 49, 54,

57, 64, 68); *211*(73); *232*(29); *232A* 142)
Dibby & Eliza *28*(206)
Dickinson *20*(83); *20A*(64:19)
Dido *28*(206); *29*(199–200)
Diligence *1*(367, 413); *11*(173–175); *24* (61:352); *29*(102); *36*(32); *64*(252); *65*(14); *243*(24)
Diligent *2*(31–32); *35*(191); *44*(81); *64*(240)
Dime *29*(15)
Dingly *29*(221)
Discovery *1*(210); *30*(19); *210*(14–15)
Dispatch *29*(39, 219); *36*(36); *64*(278, 287, 293–294, 303, 313); *135*(194); *136*(209, 212, 218–219, 225); *145* (525); *146*(3:20–21)
Dobbs *64*(260, 307)
Dogger of Yarmouth *11*(158)
Doglass *36*(32); *64*(251) *See also* Douglass.
Dolphin *2*(204); *11*(70–72, 163, 168–169); *20*(70); *20A*(63:344); *29*(184, 217); *36*(32, 34–35, 37); *57*(31:311); *63*(171); *63A*(67:107); *64*(233, 251, 255, 257–258, 266, 271, 273–274, 276, 284–286, 290, 295, 300, 307, 309, 313, 316–317); *144*(390, 405); *145*(491, 506); *146*(1:728, 747); *185*(33:475)
Domestic *29*(252)
Dorcas Ann *29*(63, 230)
Dorothea *145*(529); *146*(3:28, 30)
Dorset *1*(132); *44*(110); *44A*(355)
Dorst *2*(176, 186)
Dos Amigos *29*(52, 239); *243*(26)
Douglass *64*(258, 270); *65*(14) *See also* Doglass.
Dove *2*(27, 38, 58, 84); *4*(ser 1:23); *29*(91); *36*(32); *64*(242, 245–246, 250, 264, 268–269, 274, 276–278, 280, 287, 290, 293–294, 297, 303, 314); *198*(96); *198A–198E*
Draetvat *77*(431); *83*(5–6); *84*(181); *86*(33); *86A*(141)
Dragon *2*(40, 121, 142, 146, 161, 205–206); *11*(173, 177–178); *135*(151, 179, 208); *138*(3:490); *138A*(3:458); *141*(244); *143*(12); *144*(82, 211, 220); *145*(68, 296, 304); *146*(1:96–98, 413, 422); *147*(113, 116, 123–124); *151*(6:Spring 1955, 38;8:Summer 1956, 57); *158*(44–45); *158A*(58–59); *163*(343); *169*(13); *173*(13); *175*(179); *238*(35, 40)

Drayton 4(ser 1:71)

Dubertus 57(30:42)

Dublin Packet 28(205); 29(134)

Dublin's Prize 165(31:352–364)

Due Return 1(208, 237); 210(13, 42)

Duke of Bedford 135(157); 136(197, 201, 228); 144(252); 145(334); 146 (1:458); 151(7:Winter 1956, 39)

Duke of Cumberland 64(305)

Duke of Kingston 64(292)

Duke of Noailles 242(21:974)

Duke of Wirtemberg 132(19); 135(136, 143, 150–151, 154, 156, 159, 164, 171–172, 175, 181, 190, 212, 223, 231, 233–235); 136(214); 144(268, 288); 145 (348, 367); 146(1:475, 497); 171 (31); 175(177); 178(189)

Duke of York 12(12:159–161, 194)

Duly Ann 29(87)

Duncan 24(62:169)

Dunkirk 4(ser 1:72)

Duty 1(203, 210–211, 215, 222–224, 233, 235, 238, 251, 262); 210(15, 20, 27, 29, 38, 40, 42, 56)

E

Ea 29(24)

Eagle 20(179); 20A(65:251); 24(60:24, 349; 61:265; 66:307); 25(19–20); 29(146, 181, 207, 217); 30(20); 64 (238, 271, 305–306); 83(24); 84 (181); 86(40); 86A(155) See also de Arent.

Earl of Bute 64(278)

Earl of Donegal 238(87)

Earl of Dunmore 20(35, 90); 20A(63: 22; 64:106)

Earl of Hillsborough 238(69)

Easter 64(303)

Eastern Branch 2(205); 135(169, 172, 213, 228); 144(321); 145(423); 146 (1:585–587)

Echo 29(31)

Eclipse 29(11, 25)

Economy 29(223)

Edgar 29(257)

Edinburgh 2(11, 28, 52, 65, 98, 113, 121, 134, 154, 191); 132(11, 15, 24, 27); 136(238); 141(239, 241, 244–245); 144(181, 200, 226–227, 254, 272, 302, 318, 330); 145(261, 287, 310, 335, 351, 384, 417, 434); 146(1: 371, 402, 429, 460, 479, 521, 523, 525, 576–579, 581, 613, 615–616, 618, 620);

147(113); 151(6:Winter 1954–55, 39, Spring 1955, 37; 7:Winter 1956, 38; 8: Summer 1956, 58); 158(46); 158A (62); 163(343); 175(176, 179–182); 176(465); 182(12)

Edward 24(60:26); 25(22); 29(21, 94, 99, 106, 131, 155, 181, 218, 253, 259–260, 263, 287–288)

Edward & James 11(160)

Edward D. Douglas 29(28)

Edward Downes 243(28)

Edward Foster 29(149)

Edwin 1(202–203, 207, 240, 246, 249, 264); 29(145); 208(xxxiii); 210(6, 8, 12, 45, 51, 53, 68)

de Eendracht 2(61); 75(441); 75A (140); 76(805–806, 808); 77(54, 56, 89, 118, 120, 138, 152, 417, 435); 78 (432); 78A(338); 78B(376) See also Concord.

Eight Sons 29(213)

Elbe 243(28)

Eleanor 14(16, 21); 14A(64:256, 262); 30(18); 210(49)

Election 29(61–62)

Electra 29(186, 188)

Elias Bangor 29(13)

Elias Barger 29(270)

Elinor 1(244)

Eliza 1(60–61); 29(31, 55, 87, 179, 224, 226, 271); 64(234, 236–238, 241, 294, 306); 67(206); 138(3:555); 138A(3: 516); 144(87)

Eliza & Anne 1(54, 57–58, 61, 72)

Eliza & Mary 124(330); 124A(22)

Eliza Ann 29(93, 103, 115, 240)

Eliza Haley 29(25)

Eliza Jane 29(70, 247)

Eliza Pigotte 29(18, 105, 242)

Elizabeth 1(48, 53, 56–57, 68, 117, 231, 277, 280–281, 352, 390, 392); 2(64, 77, 99, 101, 157, 170, 177, 194, 213–214); 4(ser 1:42; ser 2: 197); 5(5, 8–9, 41, 48, 54, 68, 76, 86, 98, 152–153, 159, 164–166, 168); 11 (139); 14(21, 25); 14A(64:261, 340); 20(4, 6, 83–84, 91–92, 111–112, 154, 165); 20A(62:242, 244; 64:19–20, 108, 225–226; 65:127–128, 237–238); 28(205); 29(30, 111, 181); 35(117, 139, 144); 36(31); 44(18–22, 24–25, 27, 51–52, 55); 44A(305–308, 310, 312, 329, 332); 47(8:255–258, 261–262; 10:140–142); 57(31:311); 63(9,

Index of Ship Names, continued

11, 14, 29, 37, 47, 50, 57, 69, 90, 93, 113, 131, 138–139, 154, 174, 184, 190, 198, 205, 208, 212); *63A*(63:185, 187, 190, 281, 369, 379; 64:26, 257, 269; 65:114, 117, 539; 66:421, 522–523; 66:90, 110, 208, 214, 222, 309, 312, 316); *64*(229, 244, 250, 254–255, 260, 262, 267–269, 273, 277, 280, 282, 285, 300, 308, 316); *135*(136–137, 155, 165, 173, 193, 228–229); *141*(238, 240); *144*(128); *145*(82, 176); *146* (1:113–115, 243–245, 452, 765); *157* (150); *170*(442); *192*(255); *208* (xxxii); *210*(36); *211*(72); *217*(4: 191; 15:142); *247*

Elizabeth & Ann *1*(58, 69, 72, 76, 78); *2* (46–47, 126, 132); *5*(17, 62, 83, 128); *8*(38); *14*(22, 35); *14A*(64:336; 65: 47); *47*(8:256–259, 262–264)

Elizabeth & Anne *35*(139, 147, 154); *44* (20, 22, 24, 27–30); *44A*(308, 310, 312–314)

Elizabeth & Dorcas *44*(69)

Elizabeth & Judith *14*(30); *14A*(64: 344)

Elizabeth & Katherine *12*(12:442, 478)

Elizabeth & Mary *117*(673); *117A*(228)

Elizabeth & Sarah *11*(146); *117*(673, 677); *117A*(225–226)

Elizabeth, Anne & Catherine *124*(337); *124A*(23)

Elizabeth Bonaventure *35*(102, 108); *44* (69)

Elk *29*(47)

Elkridge *20*(155); *20A*(65:128)

Ellen *29*(143)

Elliott *2*(76); *144*(189); *145*(276); *146* (1:390); *147*(112)

Elsabeth *1*(210, 222, 245, 251, 253, 257, 259–260, 262); *208*(xxxi); *210*(15, 27, 50, 56–57, 61, 64, 66)

Emelie *255*

Emelie Marie *29*(279)

Emerald *29*(180, 249)

Emisle *165*(31:367)

Emperor Charles *77*(360)

Empress Alexander *28*(205)

Emulation *29*(120)

Encrease. *See* Increase.

Endeavor *1*(355, 362, 372, 398, 413, 418); *11*(146, 160); *12*(12:124); *64* (235, 250, 260, 282, 310); *117*(677–

678); *117A*(226); *122*(440); *123* (188); *124*(330); *124A*(22); *144* (166–167); *145*(249); *146*(1:352)

Enigheden *254*(47)

Enterprize *28*(206); *29*(57, 93, 131, 183, 189–190, 215, 223, 242); *144* (130); *145*(180, 573); *146*(1:248–249; 3:94)

Erin *27*(82); *27A*(Dec 1923:5–6; Dec 1926:29); *28*(205); *29*(11, 284)

Eros *29*(88)

l'Esperance *29*(34)

Esther *64*(242)

Esther & Sally *29*(138)

Etty *20*(10); *20A*(62:248)

Eudora *29*(29)

Eueling *57*(30:42)

Eugene *29*(42, 44, 46)

Eunice *29*(105, 145)

Euphrates *29*(18)

Europa *2*(13, 52); *141*(248); *144*(151); *145*(224, 226); *146*(1:317–319); *147* 111, 118, 123); *151*(7:Winter 1956, 39); *152*(66)

Europe *11*(182)

Euryal *166*(287)

Evergreen *29*(268–269)

Exchange *2*(124); *11*(144, 157–158, 162–163, 165–166, 68)

Exertion *29*(217)

Expectation *1*(67, 69); *2*(90–91, 129, 131, 200, 208, 215); *11*(164, 166–167); *44*(104); *44A*(350–351)

Expedition *1*(139, 393); *2*(114, 179); *44*(112); *44A*(357); *57*(30:42); *235* (170–171); *243*(23)

Experience *64*(297)

Experiment *14*(19); *14A*(64:260); *29* (27); *29*(92); *243*(27)

Express *29*(181); *145*(582); *146*(3:110–111)

den Eyckenboom *76*(824); *77*(239)

F

Factor *11*(172, 181); *29*(182, 207); *56* (334); *117*(673); *117A*(225); *199* (73)

Fair American *145*(577, 643, 657); *146* (3:45–46, 99, 178–179, 192–193); *189* (191)

Fair Hebe *145*(573); *146*(3:96)

Fair Lady *64*(308)

Fair Polly *29*(111)

Fair Trader *29*(268)

Fairfield *64*(233, 280)

Fairplay *29*(104)

Faith *2*(11, 22, 51, 72); *83*(8, 11, 16, 19, 27); *84*(181); *86*(34–35, 38, 42); *86A* (143, 146, 151, 157); *112*(21) *See also* de Trouw.

Falcon *1*(63, 142–143, 222, 233, 250, 256); *2*(176, 206, 216); *28*(206); *29* (54, 220–221); *44*(103, 113); *44A* (350, 358–359); *208*(xxix); *210*(27, 39, 54, 60)

Falls *238*(9)

Falmouth *64*(256)

Fama *29*(227); *193*(464)

Fame *27*(82); *27A*(Dec 1926:24); *29* (20, 92, 94, 99, 182, 224); *144*(414); *145*(513); *146*(1:756; 3:55, 57); *189* (340)

Fancy *64*(270)

Fane *2*(10, 47–48, 121); *135*(204); *141* (241–242); *144*(221); *145*(305); *146* (1:424); *170*(443)

Fanny *20A*(65:30); *20*(137); *29*(15–17, 183); *64*(278); *67*(205)

Fanny & Janny. *See* Fanny & Jeamy.

Fanny & Jeamy *20A*(65:33–34); *36*(39)

Fanny & Jeany *64*(288, 300)

Fanny & Jenny *20*(140, 142)

Fanny & Mary *29*(228)

Farmer's Friend *29*(27)

Favorite (Favourite) *20*(160); *20A*(65: 232); *28*(205); *29*(52, 56, 91, 148, 183); *136*(199, 217, 225, 229, 238, 245); *145*(605); *146*(3:6, 135, 137)

Fawn *29*(144)

Felicity *243*(23–26)

Fellowship *5*(56, 184); *11*(166, 168, 182); *35*(203); *44*(63); *44A*(338)

Ffenix. *See* Phoenix.

Fire of Troy *77*(237) *See also* de Brant van Trogen.

Fisher *64*(289)

Fishhawk *64*(256)

Fleetwood *20*(148); *20A*(65:121–122)

Flora *64*(277)

Florentine *243*(24)

Flower *4*(ser 2:116)

Flower of Gelderland (Guelder) *83*(5); *84*(181)

Fly *29*(181); *64*(261, 263, 283)

Flying Fish *243*(23–24)

Flying Hart *1*(243, 246, 250, 252–254); *210*(48, 50, 55–58); *214*(47); *214A* (166)

Forest *29*(33–34); *135*(134, *148*, 151, 159, 170, 189, 225); *136*(214); *144* (286); *145*(364); *146*(1:494); *154* (195)

Fortitude *24*(61:134, 138)

Fortuna *29*(49–51)

Fortune *1*(xxviii); *2*(15, 207); *5*(14, 76, 98–99, 103, 110, 113, 169, 184–185); *20*(10, 166–168, 175); *20A*(62:248; 65:238–240, 247); *30*(119, 204–207); *34*(103–131); *34A*(35); *34B*(190–191, 297–300); *34C*(79–80); *34D*(2); *35*(50); *36*(1); *44B*(121); *64*(239, 285); *145*(597, 621); *146*(3:127, 130, 157)

Foster *28*(206); *29*(138)

Foundling *28*(206)

Fountain *29*(88)

Four Sisters *35*(63)

Fox *2*(12, 65, 85, 146, 190); *29*(179, 183); *64*(275, 317); *83*(21); *84*(181); *86*(39); *86A*(152); *144*(124); *145* (168); *146*(1:231–233) *See also* de Vos.

Frances *5*(150); *44*(53–55); *44A*(331–332)

Francis *1*(277, 279); *2*(27, 170); *5*(39–40, 42, 45, 47, 54, 149, 162); *29*(93, 242, 259); *35*(121); *47*(10:143)

Francis & Ann *144*(145); *145*(207); *146* (1:292)

Francis & Dorothy *12*(12:270, 306, 518–519); *117*(677–680); *117A*(232–233); *124*(337); *124A*(23)

Francis & Elizabeth *2*(22, 28, 113, 146, 154, 205); *144*(155, 158); *145*(231, 234); *146*(1:327–328, 331–333, 409); *151*(6:Sept 1954, 37)

Francis & Katherine *64*(234)

Francis & Mary *2*(211); *11*(137, 142–143, 161–162, 164–165, 167–168, 173–174); *56*(332, 334); *199*(73)

Francis & Susan *1*(348, 416)

Francis Bonaventure *1*(203, 207–208, 212, 219–220, 224, 227, 232, 237–238, 249, 259); *210*(8, 12–13, 17, 24, 29, 33, 38, 41–43, 54, 63–64); *211*(73)

Frankland *238*(52, 55)

Franklin *29*(89–90, 219, 270)

de Frau Cathrina *189*(334)

Frederick *29*(9, 125–126, 147); *64*(260)

Frederick Augustus *145*(661); *146*(3: 196)

Free America *64*(277, 279)

Index of Ship Names, continued

Free Mason 20(82); 20A(64:18); 36 (33); 64(262); 66(184); 238(126)
Free Ocean 29(69)
Freelove 2(169, 216)
Freeman 117A(224)
French Ship 11(140); 55(388); 56 (332–333)
Friends 29(94)
Friends Adventure 63(29); 63A(63: 281); 64(235, 246, 311); 117(672); 117A(223–224, 229–230); 122(440)
Friends' Goodwill 63(69, 82–83, 88); 63A(64:269; 65:66–67, 72)
Friendship 1(145, 354, 357); 2(20, 32, 56, 65, 113, 121, 140, 181); 4(ser 1:12); 12(12:303–305, 307–308, 342, 553–555); 20(17, 37, 75); 20A(62: 321; 63:349); 21(25, 27, 56, 67); 29 (13); 35(92–93); 64(257, 301, 308); 117(674, 676); 117A(229, 231); 132 (20, 25, 31); 135(182); 138(3:307); 138A(3:290); 139(42); 139A(6:42); 139B(18); 143(7, 18); 144(54, 136, 139, 148, 171, 322, 338); 145(11, 166, 190, 195, 216, 252, 426, 441, 553); 146(1:16–17, 225, 227–230, 264–265, 267–268, 270–271, 274–275, 307–309, 356, 589–590, 642–643, 645; 3:77–78); 147(112, 115); 158(44–46); 158A(57, 60, 62); 159(23–24); 175 (181); 202(386); 202A(215); 232 (5–6); 232A(43–44); 243(28)
Fry. *See* Fly.
Fryall. *See* Trial.
Furtherance 1(231, 233, 235, 241–242, 247, 249, 251, 264); 2(171, 205); 210 (36, 39–40, 46–47, 52, 54, 56, 68); 211(73); 212(217–218); 215(136)

G

G. P. Stevenson 29(87)
Gabriel 7(74); 11(138–140, 143–144, 159, 163, 166, 168)
Galaxy 29(223)
Gale 21(28); 103(89)
Galen 29(82, 143, 229)
Gamacrau 29(240)
Ganges 29(281–282)
Garonne 29(115)
Geddis 20(36–37); 20A(63:23–24)
Geife. *See* Gift.
het Gekruijste Hart 77(412) *See also* Sacred Heart.

Gelderland 2(79)
de Geldersche Blom. *See* Flower of Gelderland (Guelder)
General Brewer 29(145–146, 150, 213–214)
General Brooks 29(221)
General Greene 29(140, 144, 149–151, 216, 219, 223)
General Griswold 29(285–286)
General Hamilton 29(180); 243(28)
General Hand 29(105)
General Jackson 29(103, 250, 277)
General Smith 29(160–161)
General Washington 29(95, 225)
General Wolfe 64(282, 292); 144(399); 145(500); 146(1:739)
Generous Friends 20(92); 20A(64:108)
George 1(124, 205–209, 212–213, 215–218, 220–223, 225–228, 231–232, 234–237, 239–241, 244–253, 256, 258, 262–265); 2(9, 41, 119, 142, 151, 203); 11 (160–162, 165, 167–168, 175–176); 12 (12:269–271, 306–307, 519); 21(30–33); 24(60:349; 61:133, 136, 138); 28 (205–206); 29(58, 79–80, 218, 242, 267); 35(161, 180); 145(567); 146 (3:91); 165(30:348, 350–352, 427–431, 433–434, 436; 31:86, 94, 195, 197, 202, 205; 32:100–103, 237–248, 351–356, 358, 370); 208(xxxi, xxxiii); 210 (10–14, 16–18, 20–23, 25–33, 36–41, 43, 45, 49, 50–58, 60–61, 66–69); 211 (71, 73); 215(132); 217(15:144);
George & Albert 28(205)
George & Anne 2(158)
George & James 64(278, 288)
George Atwood 29(144)
George Bonaventure 35(62)
George Pickett 29(49)
George Washington 29(227)
Georgetown Packet 29(207)
Georgia 21(86); 29(91)
Georgia Diana 20(145); 20A(65:118)
Georgia Packet 20(171–172, 174); 20A (65:243–244, 246)
Georgia Planter 20(76); 20A(63:350)
Georgiana 29(41)
Gertrude 29(270)
Ghent 29(140, 227)
Gift 1(206, 225, 230–231, 234, 236, 238, 245–246, 249, 254, 263); 2(46, 93, 151); 35(92); 210(11, 30, 35–36, 39, 41, 43, 46, 50–51, 53, 67); 212(217)
Gift of God 30(15)

Gilded Beaver 2(11); 83(7, 13); 84 (181); 86(33, 36); 86A(142, 147) See also de Vergulde Bever.

Gilded Otter 2(11, 21–22); 83(6, 16); 84(181); 86(33, 37); 86A(141, 149) See also de Vergulde Otter.

Ginger 64(267)

Glasgow 2(24, 64, 190, 195, 219); 15 (88); 36(38–40); 64(247, 293, 300, 304, 310, 315); 132(20); 135(143); 143(17); 144 (116); 145(151); 146 (1:204–205, 207); 147(117)

Glasgow Packet 21(57)

Gleaner 29(7, 99)

Glide 29(83)

Globe 1(119); 2(9, 17, 28, 41, 60, 74, 78, 101, 104, 136, 168, 175, 213, 215–216); 4(ser 1:25); 8(38); 14(14, 31); 14A(64:255, 345); 28(205); 63(31, (37, 71); 63A(63:283, 369; 64:271); 64(236); 66(179); 217(4:261)

Glocester 4(ser 2:156)

Gloria 36(36); 64(281)

Glorious Memory 20(96); 20A(64:112)

God Speed 1(255); 208(xxix); 210(59)

God's Gift 210(58); 211(74)

Golconda 27(82); 27A(June 1926:12–13)

Gold Huntress 29(51–52)

Golden Age 29(5, 288)

Golden Eagle 83(17, 19); 84(181); 86 (37–38); 86A(150–151) See also de Gulden Arent.

Golden Fortune 2(155)

Golden Glove 29(250)

Golden Hart 11(168)

Golden Lyon 11(139, 162–163); 12(12: 382, 405–406, 441; 13:79)

Golden Rule 20(80); 20A(63:354)

Good Friends 145(574); 146(3:94)

Good Hope 144(318); 145(415); 146 (1:573–576)

Good Intent 2(210); 4(ser 1:68); 20 (58); 20A(63:235); 29(235); 64(264, 295); 135(140, 145, 163–164, 171, 182, 199, 201–202); 144(223, 343); 145(307, 446); 146(1:426, 655–656, 658–659); 151(7:Spring 1956, 38); 175(178)

Good Return 29(20)

Good Speed 203(388)

Goodfellow 36(68)

Goodwill 11(72); 144(51, 57)

Governor 29(151, 224)

Governor Carver 29(148)

Governor Hawkins 29(57, 203)

Governor Myers 29(169–170)

Grace 64(264)

Grampus 29(102); 144(382); 145(482); 146(1:719)

Grand Corneille 29(41)

Grand Turk 29(281)

Granvil 36(39); 64(299)

la Gratitude 29(9)

Grayhound 29(7, 17, 94, 100, 130, 239–240, 257); 36(33); 64(232, 242, 262, 282, 297)

Great Hope 35(131)

Great Hopewell 1(244, 248); 4(ser 1: 26); 210(49, 53)

Great Society 11(181); 199(73)

Green Lyon 35(205)

Gregg 238(108, 110)

Griffin 2(195, 214); 5(17, 44, 54, 67, 77, 93, 109); 35(105, 113); 109(590); 110(25); 110A(60); 110B(108); 165 (32:248, 352, 360) See also Griffith.

Griffith 111(79); 165(32:248) See also Griffin.

Grizel 64(309)

Guifte. See Gift.

Guiste. See Gift.

de Gulden Arent 77(412); 196(310–311) See also Golden Eagle.

Gull 64(270, 286, 307)

Gustave 29(38)

Guyft. See Gift.

H

Halcyon 29(68)

Hale Galley 64(255)

Halifax 2(212; 64(275); 135(189–190, 215); 136(202, 220–221); 144(275, 313, 342); 145(354, 407, 445); 146 (1:482, 559–560, 562, 651, 653, 655); 175(176)

Hallan 29(228)

Hamburgh 146(3:12)

Hamburgh Packet 145(552); 146(3:76)

Hamet 29(7)

Hamilton 2(203); 132(20, 23); 139(41) 139A(5:35); 139B(11); 144(379); 145(480); 146(1:715); 151(7:Winter 1956, 39)

Hamlet 29(260)

Hammer 29(58)

Hammond 29(10, 231)

Index of Ship Names, continued

Hampshire 2(13, 22, 206); 141(242–244); 144(183); 145(262); 146(1:372, 374–375) 163(343)

Hampton 36(39); 64(264, 279, 303, 307, 310)

Hancock 29(229)

Handmaid 5(150); 35(91)

Hanna 12(12:92)

Hannah 12(12:479); 28(205); 29(61, 191, 198, 205, 288); 36(33–34); 64 (231, 249, 253, 257–258, 260, 265–266, 269, 282, 285–287, 291–292, 297, 299–300, 303, 310–311, 317); 66(183); 145 (525); 146(3:19); 185(33:475)

Hannah & Elizabeth 2(133); 60(376–377); 60A(137)

Hannah & Rebecca 29(231)

Hannibal 27(82); 27A(June 1926:2)

Hanover 64(233)

Happy Entrance 30(22)

Happy Return 1(328,331); 4(ser 1:62); 29(280); 58(447); 165(31:83, 85, 366–367, 462–463, 465–466, 468; 32:92)

Hare 28(206)

de Härinck 76(816, 821); 77(144, 414)

Haring 78(431); 78A(337); 78B(375)

Harle 2(21, 48, 70, 191, 203); 138(4:59); 143(16); 144(100); 145(121); 146(1:154, 157, 160); 151(8:Summer 1956, 57)

Harlequin 64(298)

Harmony 20(61); 20A(63:237; 27(82); 27A(Dec 1926:28–29); 29(27, 98, 277); 63(67); 63A(64:267); 145(556); 146(3:83)

Harp 29(61)

Harriet 29(24, 31–32, 86, 88, 121–122, 173); 146(3:82–83)

Harriet Baltimore 145(556)

Harriet Newell 29(147,207)

Harrison 64(277, 287, 291, 294)

Hart 2(212; 11(168–169, 177)

Harvard 29(150)

Harvey Hide 27(82); 27A(Dec 1823:6–8)

Havre Packet 29(217)

Hawk 20(168); 20A(65:241–242); 36 (37, 40); 64(255, 272, 289, 306, 311)

Hector 5(71, 98, 109); 29(7, 132–133, 247–248); 35(179–180); 71

Helen 28(205); 29(10, 103, 148, 271)

Helicon 29(10)

Henlopen 29(245)

Henricus 189(339)

Henrietta 135(151, 196, 206, 225); 141 (240); 144(341); 145(444); 146(1:648–651)

Henriquita 243(23)

Henry 29 (18, 48); 64(240)

Henry & Charles 145(555); 146(3:81–82)

Henry & Francis 113(17); 113A–113C

Henry Clay 29(84, 231)

Hepzabath 64(265, 274)

Herald 29(104, 147)

Hercules 1(xix, 220, 247–248, 255, 263) 2(99, 218); 4(ser 1:16); 5(61, 74–78, 82–85); 11(142); 29(8, 25, 119, 243–244); 30(204–208); 35(107, 114, 188); 44(69, 71, 82); 45(267); 46 (218, 223–226); 46A(750); 46B(28); 47(8:274); 146(3:54–55); 208(xxviii–xxix); 210(25, 52–53, 59, 67)

La Hermione 29(61)

Hero 20(126); 20A(64:326); 29(33, 56, 139–140); 135(215, 233); 144(363); 145(465); 146(1:696); 151(6:Spring 1955, 37; 7:Winter 1956, 39; Spring 1956, 38; 8:Summer 1956, 57)

Herring 77(237)   *See also* den Härinck.

Hesper 29(125)

Hespersus 29(11, 282)

Hibernia 27(82); 27A(Sept 1926:17–18; Dec 1926:31); 29(15, 57, 99, 206, 255, 260)

Highlander 29(239)

Higson 29(58)

Hills 29(91)

Hilsborough 64(301); 238(68)

Hind 29(279)

Hippomenes 29 (7, 99, 270)

Holland 145(548,563); 146(3:71–72,85)

Holy Oake 64(283)

de Hoop 2(28); 77(403, 434)   *See also* Hope.

Hope 1(360, 378, 392, 397); 2(22, 68, 79, 109, 142, 190); 11(139); 20(89); 20A(64:25); 29(8, 21, 52, 98, 115, 149, 217, 221–222, 239, 260); 36(35); 44A(359); 57(30:41); 64(274); 83 (17, 20); 84(181); 86(38) 86A(152); 135(152); 136(233, 237); 138(3:556, 615); 138A(3:517, 570); 143(14); 144 (88, 97, 399, 403, 411); 145(85, 109, 500, 504, 511); 146(1:116, 119–120, 142, 145, 739, 744, 753); 155(230, 247–

248); *164*(2:1–2); *185*(33:476) *See also* de Hoop.
Hope & Polly *29*(193)
Hope & Sally *29*(143, 217)
Hopeful Adventure *4*(ser 2:130)
Hopefull Katherine *11*(140)
Hopewell *1*(39, 44, 46, 49, 110, 123, 130, 144, 214, 223, 227, 230, 232–233, 237, 254, 258–259, 261, 376, 381); *2* (126, 170, 178, 204, 218); *5*(6, 9–10, 13, 49, 66, 70–71, 100, 169, 175); *7* (71); *11*(70–72, 163); *12*(12:13–14, 48–53, 89–90); *20*(136); *20A*(65:29–30); *24*(60:347); *30*(143); *35*(65, 124, 139, 158, 174, 204); *39*(33, 45); *44*(15, 17, 19, 41, 71–72, 100); *44A* (303–304, 306, 322, 347, 359); *47* (8:253–255, 271); *56*(333); *64*(239, 306); *210*(19, 28, 32, 35, 38, 42, 59, 62–63, 65); *238*(124)
Horace *29*(53)
Horatio *29*(211)
Hornet *29*(288)
Hound *12*(13:211–212, 236); *36*(33); *64*(256)
den Houttuyn *76*(827); *77*(183, 205, 273, 359, 420, 426, 433)
Howard *29*(64, 235)
Huldah *64*(264,292)
Humbird *63*(98,203); *63A*(65:122; 67:307); *64*(248)
Humility *11*(165)
Hunter *29*(20, 25, 98, 228); *30*(205)
Huntress *27*(82); *27A*(June 1926:15–16); *29*(231)
Huntsman *11*(92); *55*(388)
Hyson *29*(139)

I

Ice Plant *29*(92)
Iiana. *See* Diana.
Illinois *29*(127)
Ilsley *29*(203)
Imperial *29*(275–276)
Importer *29*(13, 270)
Increase *1*(55, 57–58, 60–61, 64); *2*(59, 115, 185); *5*(13, 34, 39–41, 46–47, 51, 98, 155, 158, 161, 166); *30*(113, 186–189); *35*(139, 148); *44*(20, 22, 24–26); *44A*(307–311); *47*(8:256, 258–261)
Indeavour. *See* Endeavor.
Independence *24*(61:137); *29* (21, 71–72, 231)

Indostan *145*(611); *146*(3:138)
Industrious Bee *63*(141); *63A*(66:525)
Industry *11*(168); *20*(35, 80); *20A*(63:22, 354); *64*(248, 250, 255, 258, 262, 265, 269, 276, 279, 288, 291, 293, 301–302, 305–307); *145*(559); *146*(3:105) *243*(23)
Infant *29*(59, 76, 165)
Ins *29*(87)
Intrepid *29*(93)
Invincible *29*(138)
Irene *155*(230, 234–236, 238, 240–246); *164*(1:162–163, 175, 210, 303–304)
Iris *29*(106, 160)
Irish Lawrell *14*(18); *14A*(64:259)
Isaac *27*(82); *27A*(Sept 1926:19); *132* (28–29); *141*(244); *144*(212); *145* (297); *146*(1:414); *151*(7:Spring 1956, 38); *163*(343)
Isabella *11*(163); *20* (159); *20A*(65:232); *21*(80); *29*(27, 37, 96); *145* (647, 661); *146*(3:183, 195–196); *248*(44–68)

J

Jabm & Jaz *36*(35)
Jackie *21*(73, 75); *232*(11); *232A*(49)
Jacob *1*(208, 227, 246–249, 251–252, 254–255, 261); *2*(113, 154); *11*(138–139, 163); *35*(58); *136*(205); *144* (215); *145*(300, 593); *146*(1:417; 3:121, 123); *151*(6:Spring 1955, 38); *155*(234); *164*(1:175); *169*(13); *210* (13, 32, 51–54, 56–59, 65); *211*(74)
Jacob & Mary *117*(678–679); *117A*(226–227)
Jamaica *2*(12, 52, 62, 67, 113, 149); *135* (193); *144*(131); *145*(181) *146*(1:251, 253–254)
Jamaica Galley *57*(30:42); *132*(25)
Jamaica Merchant *1*(317,317**, 342, 344); *11*(169)
Jamaica Packet *21* (53, 76); *64*(299, 302); *232*(10); *232A*(48)
Jamerson & Peggy *64*(268)
James *1*(88, 107, 210, 212–213, 215, 217, 232, 234–235, 239, 241, 244, 349, 373, 386, 402–403) *2*(60, 67, 88, 105, 117, 144, 147, 159, 167, 218–219); *4*(ser 1:34); *5*(5–6, 55, 60–62, 67, 84, 88–89, 107, 110, 141, 157, 177–180, 182, 186, 189); *7*(74); *11*(181); *20*(106); *20A* 64:220); *29*(26, 68, 97, 155–156, 225–226, 267); *30*(113); *35*(98, 106, 134–

Index of Ship Names, continued

135, 139, 151); *44*(31, 39, 55, 57); *44A*(315, 321, 332, 334); *47*(8:264, 270, 319); *49*(769); *144*(266); *210* (18–20, 22, 37, 39–40, 44, 46, 49); *211* (72, 74); *212*(217); *232*(8); *232A* (46)

James & Mary *2* (22); *11*(178); *64*(240) *238*(99)

James Bayley *28*(205)

James Coulter *29*(67)

James Goodwell *2*(10, 48, 76, 140, 153); *138*(3:301, 350); *138A*(3:284, 331); *141*(235); *143*(8); *145*(8, 15); *146* (1:10–11, 21–22)

James Monroe *29*(100, 263–264)

Jan Baptist *84*(181); *86*(33); *86A*(141) See also John Baptist; de St Jan Baptiste; St John Baptist.

Jane *20*(129–130); *20A*(65:22, 24); *24* (61:349); *28*(206); *29*(29, 71, 95–96, 104, 207, 217, 221, 225); *36*(33); *64* (261), *258*(340) See also Jean.

Jane & Mary *64*(240)

Jane Ann *29*(38)

Janet *36*(35); *132*(20); *135*(177, 220, 230); *141*(239); *145*(347); *146*(1: 473); *151*(6:Spring 1955, 38); *175* (175–176)

Janette Josephine *29*(256)

Jason *29*(85, 181)

Jasper *29*(217)

Jasper T. Crooker *29*(55)

Java *29*(30)

Jay *29*(28)

Jealous *243*(24)

Jean *145*(541, 561); *146*(3:62, 102–103) See also Jane.

Jeane Louise *29*(255)

Jeany *64*(286, 296, 304)

Jefferson *24*(60:240; 62:80); *29*(53, 195, 266)

Jeffrey (Jefferies) *12*(12:480–482; 13: 106–108, 145–146, 148, 176–179, 209–212); *117*(679); *117A*(228); *124* (329); *124A*(22)

Jeneffer *144*(365); *145*(467); *146*(1: 699); *182*(12)

Jenny *20*(26, 149–150); *20A*(62:330); *64*(247); *65*(15); *185*(33:475)

Jenny & Polly *20*(21–22); *20A*(62:325–326)

Jeremy *2*(199); *11*(140, 144, 177)

Jerusalem *64*(317)

Jewel *35*(65); *39*(33–34, 44, 54)

Johanes Andreas *145*(646)

Johann Andreas *146*(3:182)

Johanna *64*(295, 316)

John *1*(134, 335–336, 339); *2*(171, 196, 211–212); *4*(ser 2:140); *11*(138, 143, 158–160, 164, 167, 181–182); *20*(52, 116); *20A*(63:141; 64:316); *28*(206); *29*(104, 200); *30*(18); *36*(34); *44*(111); *44A*(356); *56*(332); *64*(230, 260, 267–270, 277, 287, 299, 309, 312–313); *67*(208); *138*(4:99); *145*(538, 543, 550); *146*(1:167–168; 3:57, 68, 74); *155*(234); *164*(1:175); *165*(30:427; 32:363)

John & Adeline *29*(57)

John & Dorothy *1*(289); *5*(123); *35* (184); *57*(31:311)

John & Edward *29*(255)

John & Elizabeth *2*(191); *12*(12:14, 48, 50, 89, 272, 307, 342, 441, 553); *132* (20, 31); *135*(178); *144*(346); *145* (448); *146*(1:665, 668–670); *151*(7: Spring 1956, 39); *175*(178, 180)

John & Francis *1*(214, 227–228, 241, 244, 250–251, 254, 263); *208*(xxix, xxxi–xxxii); *210*(19, 33, 46, 49, 55–56, 58, 67); *212*(217)

John & James *1*(360)

John & Joane *11*(167)

John & Mary *1*(377); *64*(229, 268)

John & Sarah *1*(355, 369); *29*(81–82); *44*(73–74, 76); *53*(377–379); *53A* (20); *64*(234)

John & Thomas *1*(368,404); *20*(44); *20A*(63:134); *64*(237)

John & William *2*(26–27, 67); *64*(240); *132*(10); *138*(3:501); *138A*(3:466); *139A*(5:35); *139B*(11); *143*(13); *144* (84); *145*(72); *146*(1:101, 104–105); *151*(7:Spring 1956, 38)

John Baptist *14*(31); *14A*(64:345) See also Jan Baptist; de St Jan Baptiste; St John Baptist.

John Buckley *29*(90)

John Burgwin *29*(91)

John Dickerson *29*(126, 245–246)

John Hannah *29*(223)

John Smith *29*(93)

John Williams *29*(109)

Johnson *2*(26, 68, 146, 209–210); *63* (83); *63A*(65:67); *138*(3:484); *138A*

(3:453); *143*(11); *144*(75); *146*(1:
71, 75–77); *205*
Jollif Galley *64*(237–238)
Jolly Sailor *64*(315)
Jonas *35*(107)
Jonathan *1*(201–202, 204–205, 208, 210,
216, 219–220, 222, 224, 226, 229, 233,
238, 240, 257, 259–261, 263–264); *2*
(26, 133, 140, 173, 177); *5*(25, 60–
61); *35*(56, 201); *57*(32:407); *145*
(48); *208*(xxix); *210* (5–6, 9–10, 13,
15, 20–21, 23–24, 26, 29, 31–32, 34,
38–39, 42, 45, 61, 64–65, 67–68)
Jones *29*(155)
Jones Hull *29*(66)
Jorde Colony *164*(1:209)
Joseph *1*(364, 377, 380, 382, 385, 396,
402); *2*(213); *11*(137, 144–145, 178);
12(12:518); *29*(33, 104); *29*(66)
Joseph & Ann *1*(357, 393, 402)
Joseph & Ashton *12*(12:272, 341, 552)
Joseph & Mary *1*(369); *20* (74); *20A*
63:348)
Joseph & Phoebe *27*(82); *27A*(Sept
1926:19–20)
Joseph & Sarah *64*(241)
Joseph & Thomas *225*(8)
Josiah *2*(10)
Joyce *2*(157, 191); *138*(3:414); *138A*
3:389); *144*(64–65); *145*(22); *146*
(1:37–38)
Judith *2*(24, 47, 51, 76); *12*(12:191–
192); *30*(17); *66*(179); *144*(186);
145(269); *146*(1:382); *151*(6:Sept
1954, 37)
Julia Ann *29*(270)
Juliana *29*(9)
Juliet *29*(26)
Julius Casear *29*(267)
Junius *29*(34, 63, 284)
Juno *27*(82); *27A*(Sept 1926:20–21);
28(206); *29*(92, 224); *64*(282–283);
135(158); *144*(377); *145*(478, 578,
589); *146*(1:713; 3:105–106, 120)
Jupiter *21*(88); *27*(82); *27A*(June 1926:
7–9); *29*(231–232, 234); *185*(33:475);
232(25); *232A*(138)
Justine *29*(125)

K

Kalmar Nyckel *193*(464)
Katherine *1*(249); *5*(96); *11*(136–137,
141–142, 145, 159, 167); *12*(12:307,
341); *30*(20); *35*(56); *145*(646); *146*

(3:183); *165*(31:87–89, 92, 95, 463–
466, 468, 472; 32:90, 243); *199*(73);
210(54)
Katy *29*(26); *64*(311)
Kensington *29*(74, 76)
Kent *111*(93, 99); *111A*(379)
Ketly *144*(287)   *See also* Ketty.
Ketty *132*(12); *145*(366); *146*(1:496);
151(7:Spring 1956, 38); *175*(175)
See also Ketly.
Key of Calmar *75*(438); *75A*(135)   *See
also* den Calmar Sleutel.
King Fisher *64*(283, 299)
King George *64*(239)
King of Prussia *132*(10, 26); *139A*(11–
12:84); *144*(360, 418); *145*(463, 518);
146(1:694, 762)
Kingston *36*(33); *64*(258, 260, 264, 269)
Kingston Packet *20*(87); *20A*(64:23–24)
Kinnoul *238*(113)
Kitty *29*(91); *36*(35); *64*(251, 258, 274,
297); *171*(31)
Kitty & Nelly *20*(45); *20A*(63:134)

L

L. M. Pelham *29*(259)
Laconic *258*(346)
Lady Gallatin *29*(117–118)
Lady Moore *64*(311, 313)
Lady of the Lake *29*(165); *243*(23)
Lady Washington *24*(61:137); *29*(225)
Lady's Delight *29*(124, 242)
Lamb *11*(164, 171, 174–175, 181); *14*
(13, 20, 22, 33–34, 39); *14A*(64:254,
261, 337; 65:44–45, 165); *64*(230);
117(680); *117A*(233)
Lancaster *29*(19, 283)
Lane *29*(150)
Lark *64*(246)
Lascar *29*(150)
Laura *29*(200)
Laura Ann *29*(9)
Laura Townes *243*(27)
Laurance *64*(266)   *See also* Lawrence.
Laurel *11*(140, 176), *14*(18); *14A*(64:
259); *29*(223); *55*(388); *56*(333);
143(6); *145*(532); *146*(3:32–33)
Lavinia *145*(550, 583); *146*(3:74, 111)
Lawrell. *See* Laurel.
Lawrence *29*(30, 93); *36*(34–35); *64*
(271)   *See also* Laurance.
Leader *29*(205)
Leathley *144*(307); *145*(393); *146*(1:
536–538)

Index of Ship Names, continued

Leda 28(205)
de Leide 77(203)
Leo 29(229)
Leopard 29(173); 36 (39); 145(613); 146(3:144–145)
Leslie 2(13, 56, 78–79, 216); 132(11, 15); 135(142, 154, 185, 190); 144 (216); 145(301); 146(1:419); 147 113, 124)
Letitia 20(31–32); 20A(63:18)
Lewis 29(52, 125, 272)
Liberty 20(70, 137–138); 20A(63:344; 65:30); 29(13, 91, 149); 64(276); 145 (629); 146(3:174, 177)
de Liefde 76(820) *See also* Love.
Lilly 11(157–158); 21(58–60)
Lingan 29(151)
Lion 2(41,198); 5(46, 50, 80, 101, 171); 11(141–142); 124(334); 124A(23) *See also* Lyon.
Lion's Whelp. *See* Lyon's Whelp.
Lisbon Marchant 1(355, 382)
Little Baltimore 4(ser 1:159)
Little Carpenter 238(115)
Little Cherub 29(71); 145(629, 641); 146 (3:162, 177–178)
Little Fortesque 64(257)
Little George Eyre 29(19, 79)
Little James 1(xxix); (96, 118, 169); 30 (20); 34(167–173, 175–178); 34B (242–244, 297–300); 34C(86); 34D (2); 35(55); 44B(121)
Little John 11(70–71)
Little Sarah 29(142)
Little Strength 155 (230–231, 233); 164 (1:169)
Live Oak 24(62:170)
Lively 64(289)
Liverpool 20(99); 20A(64:214); 64 (301, 311)
Liverpool Packet 29(176, 178, 207–208)
Livinia. *See* Lavinia.
Lixbos Merch^tt. *See* Lisbon Merchant.
Logan 29(105, 262); 250
Loire 29(107–108, 249, 275)
London 2(25, 119, 203); 20(34, 61, 101); 20A(63:21, 237; 64:215); 28(206); 63(45, 174); 63A(63:377; 67:110); 144(130); 145(181); 146(1:250–251) 147(117)
London Merchant 1(201–206, 216, 218– 219, 222, 227, 231, 233, 238–242, 247, 251, 260, 262, 264–265); 2(93, 142,

169); 210(5, 8–10, 21, 23–24, 27, 33, 36, 38, 42, 44, 46–47, 52, 55, 64, 66, 68); 211(73); 212(217–218)
London Packet 20(102, 104); 20A(64: 216, 218); 29(148); 64(261, 264, 276, 290, 298, 304, 314); 144(388, 395– 396); 145(489, 496); 146(1:726, 735; 3:11)
Long Robert 30(16)
Loniser 185(33:475)
Lonsdale 20(81); 20A(63:355)
Lord Dunagannon 238(104)
Lord Dunluce 238(121)
Lorenzo 28(205)
Loues Mireare 199(73)
Louisa 20(63–64); 20A(63:240); 28 (206); 135(139, 157, 182, 201, 214, 230); 144(296, 320); 145 (374, 421) 146(1:506, 581–584); 243(23–25, 28)
Louise Cecilia 29(125)
Louisiana 29(205)
Louther 138(3:444); 138A(3:417); 144 (70); 145(36) *See also* Lowther.
Love 1(109); 7(75); 12(12:193); 35 (130); 44(40); 44A(322); 47(8:271); 83(12); 84(181); 86(36); 86A(146) *See also* de Liefde.
Love & Unity 20(58); 20A(63:234)
Lovely Betsey 20(60); 64(281, 308)
Lovely Lass 20(96); 20A(64:112)
Lovely Nelly 21(63, 96)
Love's Increase 11(139–140, 157–158, 162–163)
Lovey 64(245, 247, 249, 275)
Lovonia. *See* Lavinia.
Lowther 2(27, 150); 20(106); 20A(64: 220); 143(10); 146 (1:54, 56); 232 (8); 232A(46) *See also* Louther.
Loyal George 64(239)
Loyal Judith 2(10, 13, 25, 61, 64, 79, 97, 114, 134, 153–154, 167, 189, 191); 15(88); 132(15, 18–19, 21–22, 24–26, 28–30); 135(162, 230); 138(3:487); 138A(3:456); 141(241, 243, 247); 143(12, 19); 144(79, 136–137, 141, 153–154, 159); 145(62, 192, 200, 228, 237); 146 (1:87, 89, 91, 265, 267, 269, 270, 272, 282–283, 285, 323–325, 334, 336–338); 147(108, 111, 118); 151(6:June 1954, 40, Sept 1954, 37, Winter 1954–55, 39); 152(65); 159 (24); 163(342–343)
Loyal Subject 12(12:442)
Loyalty 14(11, 21); 14A(64:166, 262)

Lucretia *29*(57); *64*(249, 300)

Lucy *29*(55, 218); *36*(35); *64*(245, 247, 249–250, 258, 263, 267, 273, 303, 306)

Luminary *29*(21)

Lunion *29*(121)

Lutus *11*(72)

Lydia *2*(15, 27, 47, 49, 67–68, 77, 103, 127, 144, 154, 160, 181, 191, 209); *29* (52, 142); *20A* (63:141; 65:35); *29* (138); *64*(265, 274, 278, 290, 298, 303, 308–309, 313); *135*(154, 191, 215, 231); *141* (248); *145*(194–195, 211, 240, 257, 302); *146*(1:273–274, 276–278, 300–302, 340–342, 364, 420; 3:13–14); *147*(124); *151*(7:Spring 1956, 39; 8:Summer 1956, 57); *152* (66); *158*(43); *158A*(56)

Lydia & Mary *29*(64)

Lyon *1*(213); *2*(61,177); *4*(ser 1:59); *5*(47, 53–54, 66, 155); *11*(141, 157); *29*(41–42); *30*(388); *35*(62, 85–86, 92, 94, 99, Appendix); *39*(47–48, 106–107); *64*(287); *123* (64, 83, 85); *144* 138–140, 161, 177); *208*(xxviii); *210* (18) *See also* Lion.

Lyon's Whelp *5*(35–37, 147); *35*(61)

M

M. Hope *29*(207)

M'Donough *29*(64, 104)

Madiera Packet *29*(154)

Madison *29*(92, 198)

Maecht van Enchuysen *78*(431); *78B* (375)

Magdalina *243*(25–26)

Magdeline *21*(44)

Magna Charta *20*(69); *20A*(63:343); *232*(5); *232A*(43)

Magnet *29*(104, 111, 134–135, 240, 280)

Maine *29*(82)

Mairmaid. *See* Mermaid.

Malley *138*(3:304); *138A*(3:287)

Malvina *29*(181–182)

Manhattan *29*(16, 263) *106*

Marblehead *64*(242)

Mercello *29*(252)

Marcus Hill *28*(205–206)

Marcy & Sarah *57*(30:41)

Marechal d'Estrées *242*(21:970)

Margaret *1*(154, 205); *2*(118, 188); *24* (60:26, 348); *25*(21); *28*(206); *29* (13, 27, 30, 33, 53, 87, 94, 189, 195, 222); *36*(36); *44*(66); *64*(281); *124* (330); *124A*(22); *135*(185); *145*(618,

631); *146*(3:153, 157, 163); *191*(9); *210*(10); *243*(27–28); *243A*(28)

Margaret & John *1*(203, 209, 211, 215, 218, 220, 222, 226, 231, 233, 235, 240–242, 246, 248–253, 255–256, 261, 265); *210*(8, 14, 16, 20, 22, 25, 27, 31, 36, 39–40, 45–47, 51, 53–57, 60, 65–66, 69); *211*(73); *212*(217–218); *215*(125)

Margaret & Mary *20*(34); *20A*(63:21); *232*(4); *232A*(42)

Margaret Wright *29*(228)

Margaretto *243*(28)

Margery *30*(188)

Margett & John. *See* Margaret & John.

Margiana *243*(28)

Margrett. *See* Margaret.

Marguiriet *243*(26)

Maria *24*(61:267); *29*(10, 20–22, 25, 70, 88, 99–100, 179, 235–236, 272); *145*(587); *146*(3:116–117)

Maria Ann *29*(263)

Maria Caroline *29*(278)

Maria Duplex *27*(82); *27A*(Dec 1926: 25)

Maria Elizabeth *145*(616); *146*(3:147)

Maria Theresa *29*(131)

Marie *242*(15:453)

Marigold. *See* Marygold.

Marine *27*(82); *27A*(Dec 1926:26) *29* (159)

Marion *29*(112)

Marius *29*(194)

Market Gardner *2*(22, 72) *See also* de Moesman.

Marlborough *2*(77, 200, 204); *15*(88); *20*(93, 169); *20A*(64:109, 65:242); *21*(47, 49, 93); *57*(31:310); *63*(11); *63A*(63:187); *132*(22); *144*(145); *145* (207); *146*(1:293–295); *147*(111,115, 118); *158*(44); *158A*(57)

Marmaduke *1*(203, 210, 216, 225, 230–231, 234, 242, 251, 254); *35*(59); *210* (7, 15, 20–21, 30, 35, 37, 39, 47, 56, 59); *212*(218)

Marmion *29*(85)

Mars *24*(60:24); *29*(30, 120)

Martha *29*(17, 132, 224, 250, 274); *64* 233, 240); *111*(102); *111A*(379); *117*(673); *117A*(225); *146*(3:55); *165*(31:92, 365–367, 461–463, 465, 467; 32:89, 103, 351); *189*(340)

Martha & Hannah *57*(30:40)

Martha & Sarah *11*(166, 174–175)

Martin *2*(137, 139); *5*(8, 11); *35*(201)

Index of Ship Names, continued

Mary *1*(348, 358, 362–363, 368, 370–371, 374, 380, 387); *2*(10, 24, 68, 78, 103, 114, 164, 171); *4*(ser 1:41–42); *11*(162–163, 166, 176–177); *12*(12: 91–92, 162, 191, 193–194, 212); *20*(32, 59, 105, 118, 133, 165); *20A* (63:19–20; 64:219–220, 318; 65:26, 238); *24* (61:350); *27*(82); *27A*(June 1926: 13–14); *28*(205); *29*(7, 13, 15, 29–30, 74, 94, 139, 142, 147–148, 224–225, 241, 263, 279–280); *57*(31:310); *64* (234, 238, 241, 251, 256–257, 260, 267, 272, 293, 300, 306); *138*(3:489, 559, 647); *138A*(3:457, 519, 597); *144*(81, 92, 99, 153); *145*(66, 100, 118, 227, 533, 535, 537, 554, 557, 567); *146*(1:93–95, 130, 132–133, 151–152, 322; 3:32, 35, 41–42, 78–79, 83, 85, 90); *147* (107–108, 116); *151* (7:Winter 1956, 38); *160*(150); *189*(188) *See also* Mary Galley.

Mary & Abagail *57*(31:311)

Mary & Ann *20*(126); *20A*(64:326); *222*(82–86)

Mary & Aschsah Ann *29*(74, 203)

Mary & Elizabeth *20*(34); *20A*(63:21–22)

Mary & Hannah *20*(110); *20A*(64:224); *232*(9); *232A*(47)

Mary & James *1*(202, 244, 251–252, 257); *208*(xxix–xxxi); *210*(7, 49, 55, 57, 61)

Mary & Jane *35*(105)

Mary & Joane *2*(177); *11*(162, 166–167)

Mary & John *2*(65, 102, 144, 196, 203); *5*(19, 21–22, 26, 29–30, 32, 34–35, 37, 61, 63, 140–142, 144, 146–147, 178–180); *30*(15); *35*(87, 110); *36*(5); *39* (47–49, 100, 102, 106); *41; 44*(68–71); *45*(267)

Mary & Martha *29*(141)

Mary & Nancy *29*(146)

Mary & Sally *29*(38)

Mary & Sarah *1*(350, 356, 386, 393, 414); *2*(170); *136*(240); *144*(345); *145*(447); *146*(1:660–663, 665)

Mary & Susan *29*(96)

Mary Ann *2*(109,188); *5*(115, 120, 123, 164–165, 183); *20*(35); *20A*(63:22); *29*(28–30, 38, 67–68, 96–97, 226); *44*(48); *63*(15, 17, 214); *63A*(63: 191, 269; 67:318); *64*(235); *243*(27)

Mary Ann Margaret *1*(257); *208*(xxxi); *210*(62)

Mary Anne *35*(181)

Mary Galley *144*(184); *145*(265); *146* 1:376–377) *See also* Mary.

Mary Margaret *1*(203, 220, 244, 263); *208*(xxviii–xxix); *210* (8, 25, 49, 67)

Mary Maria *243*(28)

Mary Providence *1*(246, 250); *210*(51, 55)

Mary Rose *29*(25, 27); *35*(202)

Mary William *11*(177)

Marygold *1*(204–205, 207, 216, 225, 235, 237, 240, 248, 252, 264); *2*(46); *4*(ser 1:52); *208*(xxxiii); *210*(9–10, 12, 20, 30, 40, 42, 45, 53, 57, 69)

Maryland *29*(89)

Maryland Merchant *2*(167); *11*(143, 160–161, 164–165, 167–168, 172, 174–175, 182); *199*(73–74)

Maryland Packet *64*(306)

Maryland Planter *20*(133–134); *20A* (65:26, 28)

Massachusetts *64*(289, 315, 317)

Massasoit *29*(173–174)

Mast Fleet *63*(198); *63A*(67:222)

Matilda *29*(55, 93)

Matthew *1*(80); *2*(75, 141, 165, 167–168); *44*(107); *44A*(353)

Matty *21*(33–34); *102–1*(204); *102–1A* (23); *185*(33:475)

Mayflower *1*(xxiv, 27, 352, 394); *2*(27); *4* (ser 1:33); *5*(30, 39, 47, 50, 55, 59, 62, 77, 82, 98–99, 102, 104, 106–108, 111, 121, 133, 137, 170, 184–186); *30* (188, 281, 388); *33*(399); *33A*(48, 52); *33B*(56); *33C*(166–195); *33D* (66); *33E*(101); *33F–33G; 34*(7–8, 25–99); *34B*(183–186, 297–300); *34C* (20–22); *34D*(1); *35*(47, 64–65); *37; 39*(24, 33, 35, 45, 106, 108); *44B*(115–116); *64*(230–231, 240)

Maylar *64*(308)

Mechanic *24*(62:168); *29*(104, 114); *145*(662); *146*(3:197)

Medford *29*(87)

Melita *29*(195)

Mentor *29*(38)

Mercator *29*(13); *29*(112)

Merchant *11*(176)

Merchant Adventurer *35*(205)

Merchant's Hope *1*(116); *2*(55, 71, 90–91, 134, 190); *44A*(359); *217*(4:190; 15:142)

Mercury 2(10, 51, 61, 76, 168); 29(31, 148, 217); 64(238, 247, 259); 138(3: 642); 138A(3:593); 143(15); 144 (98); 145(113); 146(1:146, 149–150); 153(121)

Mermaid 20(39–40, 157–158); 20A(63: 26; 65:130, 132); 29(230–231); 64 261, 295)

Merryland Merchant. See Maryland Merchant.

Meta 29(64); 248(98–114)

Meteor 29(217)

Metoka 258(339, 341–347)

Mexico 28(205); 246

Middleton 64(232)

Milford 29(104)

Milledgeville 29(57, 143, 216, 221)

Millen Den Ersten 29(178)

Miller 29(149, 220, 223)

Milo 29(111, 288)

Minehead 64(291)

Minerva 2(220); 20(23–26, 45, 74, 142); 20A(62:327–330; 63:134, 348; 65:116); 28(205); 29(66, 148, 242); 63(32, 150, 186); 63A(63:284; 66:534; 67: 210); 135(166, 185, 193, 210, 213); 136(210, 215, 237); 139(42); 139A(6: 42); 139B(18); 141(246); 144(381, 383, 388, 390, 394, 400); 145 (482, 485, 489, 492, 495, 500, 555); 146(1: 718, 721, 726, 729, 733, 739; 3:79–80); 151(6:Spring 1955, 37; 8:Summer 1956, 58); 152(64); 185(33:475)

Mirror 29(116)

Missouri 29(38, 78)

de Moesman 77(126, 131, 193, 430); 83 6, 11–12); 84(181); 86(33, 35–37); 86A(141, 145, 147–148) See also Market Gardner.

Moffat 29(195)

Mohawk 24(60:162)

Molly 2(13, 25, 52, 73, 114, 120, 124, 126); 20(58, 63, 73); 20A(63:234, 240, 347); 36(34); 63(96); 63A(65: 120); 64(252–254, 259, 262, 265, 291, 295–297, 302–304, 308–309, 311, 314–317); 141(236); 144(52, 106, 149–150); 145(9, 135, 218, 221, 555, 567, 582); 146(1:12–13, 173–174, 310–315; 3:82, 111); 147(111, 114–115); 151(6:Sept 1954, 37, Winter 1954–55, 39); 152(65); 158(44, 46); 158A (58, 61)

Monai 243(27)

Monomia 21(70–72)

Montague 28(206); 144(414); 145 (514); 146(1:757)

Montgomery 29(31)

Moravia 145(602)

Morning Star 2(88); 29(211–212); 117 (680); 117A(233); 123(95, 105, 117, 119, 125, 150, 166, 209, 263); 124 (329); 124A(22); 144(404); 145 (504); 146(1:744)

Morris 29(86)

Mortonhouse 2(47, 114, 124, 154, 209); 138(3:346, 390); 138A(3:327, 367); 143(8–9); 144(55, 58); 145(12, 15); 146(1:17–19, 23, 25–26)

Mount Bay 28(206)

Mount Vernon 29(91–92, 254)

Mountserrat Merchant 11(169)

Mulberry 14(21); 14A(64:262); 64(296)

Murrey (Murray) 64(247, 249)

Muscliffe 2(26); 135(188); 144(172); 145(253); 146(1:358)

Mynheer van Barckel 146(3:3)

Myrtilla 135(170); 144(372); 145(474); 146(1:707)

Mystic 29(221)

N

Nachen 30(17)

Nancy 2(12, 20, 26, 191, 203, 209–210); 20(17, 99–100, 132, 148, 163–164); 20A(62:321, 64:115, 214; 65:25–26, 121, 235–236); 28(205); 29(9, 15–17, 27, 64, 87, 111–112, 170, 197–198, 247, 280); 36(32, 34–35); 64(248, 252, 257, 259, 261, 264, 266, 273, 281, 287, 289–290, 292, 297, 301–302, 304, 306–307, 309, 313–314, 316); 135(135, 137, 144, 162, 169, 171, 174–175, 177, 180, 183, 188–189, 196–197, 199, 202, 204, 218, 222, 228); 144(124, 238, 256, 282, 323, 415); 145 (164, 321, 337, 361, 427, 491, 515); 146(1:226–227, 229, 442, 462, 491, 591–593, 595, 757; 3:103–104); 165(32:352, 354); 175 (183); 176(464); 238(76, 80); 243 (24)

Nancy & Friendship 144(122)

Nancy & Mary 29(221)

Nancy & Sucky 144(387); 145(489); 146(1:725)

Nancy Mumm 4(ser 1:56, 58)

Nansimum. See Nancy Mumm.

Index of Ship Names, continued

Nassau *64*(295); *145*(524); *146*(3:18–19)

le Nasseau *224*(29)

Natchez *29*(191)

Nathaniel *1*(349, 363, 366, 368, 388, 405, 411, 415); *2*(88); *11*(159); *60*(378)

Nautilis *28*(205); *29*(150)

Nellam *64*(260)

Nelly *64*(254, 260)

Nelly Frigate *20*(140); *20A*(65:33)

Neptune *1* 201–203, 206–207, 209, 215, 230, 240, 242, 245, 247, 249–250, 253–255, 258, 354, 360, 364, 366, 372, 390, 397, 408, 412); *2*(62, 190, 205); *11* (140, 158); *20*(69, 97–98, 100, 146); *20A*(63:343; 64:113–114, 214; 65: 119–120); *24*(60:26); *25*(20–21); *29* (180, 213, 283); *35*(108, 203); *44*(61–62, 69); *44A*(337); *57*(30:42); *63* (83, 197); *63A*(65:67; 67:221); *64* 230, 239–240, 286, 304); *132*(18–19, 26, 29); *135*(144, 170, 178, 181, 183, 186, 202, 209, 212, 214, 216, 232); *136* (202, 204, 207, 210, 212, 216, 219, 221–225, 228, 231–234, 236, 238–239, 246, 249, 253–254, 256, 258); *144*(175, 259, 261, 283, 308, 332, 348–349, 390, 413); *145*(256, 341–342, 362, 394, 435, 450–451, 491, 513); *146*(1:362, 466–467, 492, 538, 540, 542–543, 545, 620, 622, 624, 626, 671–675, 677–679, 681, 728, 756); *151*(7:Winter 1956, 38, Spring 1956, 39; 8:Summer 1956, 57); *158*(43); *158A*(57); *175*(175); *176*(465); *210*(6, 8, 11–12, 14, 20, 35, 45, 47, 50, 52, 54–55, 57–59, 62); *211*(71, 74); *212*(217–218)

Neptune's Barge *29*(215)

Nereus *29*(85)

Nesesidad *243*(26)

Nevis Adventure *11*(136–137, 142–143)

Nevis Merchant *2*(169, 175); *11*(144, 155, 159–160, 164, 166, 169–172, 174)

New Bean *29*(7–8)

New England Galley *63*(110); *63A*(65: 536)

New England Merchant *11*(164, 167, 173, 181)

New Industry *63*(179); *63A*(67:203)

New Packet *29*(147)

New Polly *64*(267)

New Swallow *64*(248, 254)

New York *4*(ser 1:89); *145*(581); *146* 3:109–110); *243*(23, 27–28)

Newbury *64*(270)

Newburyport *29*(167–168)

Newfound Land Merchant *11*(140); *55* (388)

Newmarket *20*(106); *20A*(64:220); *232* (8); *232A*(46)

Newry Assistance *185*(33:475)

Newton *145*(608); *146*(3:140)

Niagara *28*(206); *29*(203–204)

Nicholas *4*(ser 2:160); *20*(37); *20A*(63: 24)

Nicholas & Rebecca *1*(376, 406)

Nicholson 4 (ser 1:61)

Nightingale *30*(19)

Nimrod *29*(104, 182, 185–186, 243)

Noah *1*(204); *208*(xxix); *210*(9)

Nord America. *See* North America.

Norden *254*(24)

Norfolk *20*(76); *20A*(63:350)

Norris *2*(56); *138*(3:457); *138A*(3: 429); *139*(39); *139A*(5:30); *139B*(6); *144*(71); *145*(37); *146*(1:57–58)

den Norske Klippe *254*(33)

North America *29*(48); *145*(528); *146* (3:24–25)

North Briton *64*(299)

Northumberland *258*(354–357, 359–367)

Norwich *4*(ser 1:87)

Nova Scotia *64* (272–273, 275–276, 280, 282, 284, 287, 289–293, 295–296, 298, 301–302)

Nova Scotia Packet *36* (37–39)

Nuestra Ira *243*(24)

Numa *24*(60:23)

Nymph *29* (61, 283)

O

Oak Tree. *See* den Eyckenboom.

Oake *11*(172)

Ocean *29*(117, 258, 267); *146*(3:106)

Octavia *29*(32, 227)

Ohio *29*(280)

Oley Frigett *57*(31:311)

Olive *29*(215); *63*(113); *63A*(65:539); *64*(276, 290, 292, 294)

Olive Branch *11*(169); *20*(139–140); *20A*(65:33); *29*(15, 109, 146, 195, 220); *64*(275)

Olive Tree *11*(165, 175–176)

Oliver *2*(93); *131*(1:101); *144*(99–100) *145*(119); *146*(1:152–154); *151*(7: Spring 1956, 38)

Only Daughter 29(58, 228)
Only Son 28(206); 29(148)
Onslow 29(105)
Ontario 28(29:205–206)
Oracle 29(223)
Orient 28(205–206); 257
Orion 29(9)
Orison 29(257)
Orizimbo 29(119–120)
Orlando 27(82); 27A(June 1926:9) 145 (648); 146(3:185, 187)
Orleans 29(127)
Oryza 29(175)
Osgood 2(203) 132(21); 135(139, 145, 159, 161, 166, 176–177, 196, 219, 224, 235–236); 144(241); 145(323); 146 (1:445); 151(8:Summer 1956, 57); 169 (13); 170(442)
Ossian 28(206)
Ossipee 29(65–66)
Oswego 29(85)
de Otter 77(282, 308–309, 422, 424, 428, 433); 83(10, 15); 84(181); 86(35, 37); 86A(144, 149)
Owner's Adventure 2(216)
Owners Advice 117(679); 117A(228)

P

P. S. 29(24, 152)
Pacific 29(283)
Packet 29(57, 243)
Packet Eliza 29(229)
Paliena 144(187)
Paliena & Margaret 144(188)
Pallas 20(76); 20A(63:350); 29(56); 144(354–355); 145(457, 576); 146(1: 687; 3:46–47, 98); 189(193); 232(6); 232A(44)
Palofax 29(142)
Paoli 64(315)
Paragon 29(215, 217)
Parnassor 29(13)
Patience 1(253, 255); 2(10, 113, 119, 149, 154, 181, 191, 200, 205, 219); 11 141, 181–182); 20(95); 20A(64:111); 36(30–31); 64(243); 66(179); 135 (133–135, 140, 143–146, 154, 156–157, 163–164, 166–167, 171, 176, 178, 182, 193–198, 201, 204–206, 210, 218, 220, 226, 233–234, 236); 136(199, 212, 228, 257); 139A(11–12, 84); 141(239, 241); 144(206, 223–224, 249, 304); 145(269, 292, 307, 331, 386); 146(1: 383–384, 387–388, 407, 426, 455, 526– 527, 529–531); 151(6:June 1954, 40, Winter 1954–55, 39, Spring 1955, 38; 7:Spring 1956, 38); 169(13); 170 (442); 174(9); 175(181); 199(74); 208(xxix); 210(57, 60)
Patience & Judith 64(236)
Patience & Margaret 132(28); 135 (208); 145(274); 146(1:386–338)
Patient 20(40); 20A(63:27)
Patriot 29(175)
Patsey Rutledge 136(197, 229); 145 (524, 526, 534); 146(3:6, 16–17, 22, 24, 34, 38, 48, 104)
Patty 24(60:241); 27(82) 64(295)
Patty & Peggy 144 (417); 145(517); 146(1:760)
Patty & Sally 29(253)
Patuxent 20(64, 145); 20A(63:241; 65; 119)
Paul 1 (50, 103); 2(28, 107, 132, 151, 161, 172); 44(102); 44A(349); 217 (4:61)
Paula 243(23–25)
Pauline 248(77–92)
Peace & Pleanty 21(54–55); 64 (251)
Peacock 29(267)
Pear Tree 83(5); 84(181) *See also* de Pereboom.
Pearl 11(143); 64(260); 238(85); 243 (26)
Pegasus 29(49, 74)
Peggy 2(191, 195); 4(ser 1:86); 20(18, 20); 20A(62:322, 324); 36(32); 64 (249, 252, 262, 267, 275, 280, 304);132 (22); 135(136, 140, 146, 148, 190, 197, 207, 215, 219, 226, 229, 234, 237); 136 (244, 246); 139(40); 139A(5:33–34); 139B(10); 144(310, 337); 145(397, 440, 542, 549, 575); 146(1:545–548, 550, 636, 638–641; 3:61, 72–73, 95); 185(33:475–476)
Peggy & Hannah 36(35); 64(274)
Peggy Stewart 20(90); 20A(64:106)
Pelican 64(231)
Pell (Pill) Packet 64(253, 266)
Pembroke 64 (256)
Penelope 29(131, 181); 243(28)
Penguin 29(143)
Penn 185(33:475)
Pennsylvania 2(28, 49, 195); 24(60:27) 29(70); 143(11); 144(73, 350); 145 45, 453, 575, 587, 607); 146(1:681– 682; 3:96, 98, 115–116, 137)
Pennsylvania Farmer 238(125)

Index of Ship Names, continued

Pennsylvania Merchant 2(61, 76, 97, 191); *132*(25); *138*(3:440, 483, 557); *138A*(3:413, 452, 518); *141*(245); *144* (66, 89–90); *145*(25, 91); *146*(1:42, 45–46, 66, 68–69, 121, 124–125); *147* (108); *152*(62)

Pennsylvania Packet *15*(90); *20*(143–145); *20A*(65:116, 119); *144*(383, 394, 404); *145*(484, 495, 505); *146* (1:720, 733, 746); *151*(6:June 1954, 40, Winter 1954–55, 39); *185* (33:476); *187*(379)

Percival 29(110)

Perseverence 27(82); *27A*(June 1926:3); 29(30–31, 69)

Persia 29(55)

Perth Amboy 2(56, 66); *144*(104); *145* (130)

Peter *4*(ser 2:142–143); *11*(169)

Peter & Anthony 223(153–155); *224*(14)

Peter & Phillip 57(30:42)

Peter Bonaventure *1*(43, 47, 51); 2(152); *44*(101–102); *44A*(348–350)

Phanton 29(26, 91)

Pheba. *See* Phoebe.

Phil Tabb 29(138)

Philadelphia 29(63, 193–194)

Philadelphia Packet *145*(535–536); *146* (3:34–35, 41–42, 44–45, 48); *189*(187, 190, 193)

Philedini 29(87)

Philenia 29(21)

Philippe *242*(15:68)

Phillip *1*(94); 2(80, 131, 179); 29(86); *30*(188, 288, 303); *112*(15, 22); *217* (3:184)

Philotaxe 29(228)

Phoebe 29(93, 95); *144*(402); *145*(503); *146*(1:742)

Phoenix *1*(213); 2(56, 65, 67, 119–120, 154, 191, 200, 210); *11*(142, 159–160); *15*(88); *64*(245, 252, 264, 270, 290, 295, 305, 314); *117*(673); *117A*(225); *132* (10, 15, 22, 25); *135*(151–153, 158, 165, 167, 170, 185, 197, 204, 212–213, 218, 220, 225, 230) *136*(197, 199–200, 202–204, 206, 208–216, 219–224, 226, 228, 230–232, 234–239, 241–245, 247–249, 253, 255–257); *139*(39, 41); *139A*(5: 30, 36; 6:44); *139B*(6, 12, 20); *141* (239); *144*(163, 169, 202–203, 236, 262–263, 292, 297, 334); *145*(244, 251, 289, 318, 343, 370, 375, 437); *146*(1:

346, 355, 404, 439, 469, 501, 507, 626, 629, 633, 636); *147*(112, 119, 123) *151* 6:June 1954, 40, Sept 1954, 37; 7:Winter 1956, 38–39, Spring 1956, 38–39; 8: Summer 1956, 58–59); *154*(195); *171* (31); *175*(176, 178, 182–183); *176* (464); *185*(33:475); *208*(xxviii); *210* (18)

Pide Cowe. *See* Pied Cow.

Pied Cow *1*(106, 110); 2(135, 148); *30* (103, 119); *35*(174); *44*(38, 41); *44A* 320, 322); *47*(8:269, 271)

Pilgrim 29(200, 202)

Pill Packet. *See* Pell Packet.

Pilot 29(207)

Pineapple *64*(235)

Pink 29(98)

Pizarro 29(98)

Plain Joan *1*(78); 2(47, 73, 139, 155, 188); 5 (31); *38*(248); *217*(2:212)

Plaisance 2(149, 209); *138*(3:485); *138A*(3:454); *144*(77); *145*(52); *146* (1:78, 81–82)

Plantacon *1*(360, 372, 381, 385, 390–391, 398, 403)

Plantation *30*(20)

Planter *1*(43, 45, 47–48, 50, 53, 55–56); 2(67, 95, 123, 127, 142); *4*(ser 1:41); 5(1–2, 6, 65, 69–70, 92, 112, 168); *11* (141, 162); *14*(22); *14A*(64:263); *20* (29–30); *20A*(63:16, 18); 29(15, 33, 181, 213, 226); *30*(143); *35*(108, 139–140); *38*(249); *44*(15–21, 69); *44A* (303, 305–307); *47*(8:253–257); *56* (333)

Planters Adventure *238*(40)

Platacon. *See* Plantacon.

Plato 29(166)

Pleasant 2(49, 120, 161, 205, 208); *138* (3:498); *138A*(3:465); *144*(83); *145* (70); *146*(1:99–101)

Pleasure *35*(60)

Plough 5(60, 102, 105)

Plough of Woolwich *35*(94)

Pocohantas 29(95, 143, 166)

Polly *15*(90); *20*(59); *20A*(63:236); 29 (104); *36*(33–34, 40); *64*(246–247, 249, 259, 262, 264, 266–269, 272, 279–280, 285, 289, 297, 299, 308, 310, 312, 314, 316); *136*(201); *139*(41–42); *139A*(6:37–39); *139B*(13–15); *144*(357, 369, 376); *145*(459, 471, 477, 541, 567, 583); *146*(1:690, 703, 712; 3:61, 82, 90,112); *151*(7:Spring 1956, 39); *232* (5); *232A*(43)

Pomona 165(32:369–370)
Poppett 36(38); 64(294)
Port Royal 2(39)
Portia 29(225)
Portland 24(60:24); 29(19)
Portsmouth 1(367)
Post Boy 29(222)
Postilion 1(402)
Potomac 20(158); 20A(65:132)
Potomac Merchant 12(13:78)
Potowmack. See Potomac.
Pratt 64(282, 292, 299, 303)
President 24(61:350); 29(21, 88); 135 (137, 183, 198, 201, 211, 213, 220); 136(199); 144(281); 145(360); 146 1:489)
Primrose 1(114); 2(14, 18, 28, 41, 72, 137, 140, 147); 8(38); 11(159, 163, 165, 169, 180–181), 38(248); 217(4: 189)
Prince 12(12:309, 341, 343; 13:13)
Prince Eugene 4(ser 1:64)
Prince Henry 238(11)
Prince Madoc 29(93, 253–254)
Prince of Brazil 28(206)
Prince of Orange 64(283)
Prince of Wales 2(191); 64(261); 144 (366); 145(468); 146(1:700); 151(8: Summer 1956, 58)
Princes of Portugal 64(236)
Princess Augusta 2(92, 126); 135(217); 138(4:72); 143(16); 144(102); 145 (126); 146(1:162, 164–165); 151(7: Spring 1956, 38)
Princess Caroline 20(81)
Priscilla 2(20, 154, 190, 203); 63(157); 63A(67:93); 64(246, 282, 288, 300); 135(234); 136(226, 231, 233–235, 246, 255); 144(196, 240); 145(283, 322); 146(1:397, 443)
Progress 258(339,342)
Prophet Daniel 35(56)
Prosperity 11(181); 29(196); 57(31: 310); 64(241); 64(278)
Prosperous 1(203, 205, 207, 214, 220, 230, 246, 248, 348, 352, 363, 384, 395, 400, 405, 415, 418); 2(80, 85, 109, 140); 11(158); 208(xxix, xxxiv); 210 (7, 10, 12, 19, 25, 35, 51, 53)
Protection 27(82); 27A(June 1926:3–5; Dec 1926:25–26)
Providence 1(243, 247, 251–252, 259, 352–353, 377, 380–381, 396, 401); 4 (ser 1:65); 11(92, 94, 157, 174–175,

180); 12(12:269–270, 518–519); 30 19, 22); 36(33); 64(231, 255, 261); 117(679); 117A(227–228); 124(333); 124A(22–23); 208(xxxiii); 210(48, 51, 55–56, 63); 214(47); 214A(166)
Prudence 24(61:265)
Prudence & Mary 1(348, 369, 380, 383, 389, 406, 411, 416)
Purchase 64(314)
de Purmerender Kerck. See de Purmerlander Kerck.
Purmerland Church 83(19, 22); 84 (181); 86(38–39); 86A(151, 153); 112(4) See also de Purmerlander Kerck.
de Pumerlander 77(272)
de Purmerlander Kerck 195(69–70 & photostat illus. opp 68); 196(310–311)
Pyrennes 29(227)

Q

Queen Ann 57(31:311)
Queen Elizabeth 2(47); 143(18); 144 (120); 145(160); 146(1:216, 218–219); 147(122)
Queen Margaret 2(135)
Queen of Denmark 2(178, 217); 132 (25); 135(148); 136(237, 240); 141 (239); 144(265, 294, 301); 145(346, 372, 382); 146(1:472, 504, 516, 518–521); 182(12)
Quiroga 29(90)

R

Rachel 20(170); 20A(65:243); 24(60: 26); 29(183–184, 210); 146(1:409)
Radius 27(82); 27A(Nov 1924:11); 29 (255, 268)
Rainbow 2(114); 11(93, 168, 173); 36 (35, 39); 55(388); 64(265, 272, 277, 281, 300, 306, 311); 146(3:51); 189 (336)
Rajah 67(209)
Raleigh 27(82)
Rambler 29(11, 224)
Randolph 20(37); 20A(63:24)
Ranger 29(183, 221); 36(33); 64(247–248, 250, 256, 260, 268, 271, 279, 292, 294–295, 297–298, 301, 303, 306–308, 311, 313, 315–316)
Ranier 2(68, 114); 144(209); 145(294); 146(1:411)
Rathornis 56(332)

Index of Ship Names, continued

Rawley *135*(155, 172, 186–187); *146* (1:499)

Rea Galley *185*(33:475)

Rebecca *1*(50, 54, 369, 385, 390, 392, 396, 401, 407, 413, 416, 418); *2*(215); *4*(ser 1:31); *20*(96); *20A*(64:112); *30*(19); *35*(125, 139, 160); *44*(19–20); *44A*(306–307); *47*(8:255–256); *64*(240, 278, 313); *117*(680); *117A* (232); *124*(335); *124A*(23); *145* (613); *146*(3:145, 147); *165*(32:356–357, 359–366, 370)

Rebecca Ann *29*(274)

Rebecca Sims *29*(64)

Recover *29*(98, 183)

Recovery *1*(375, 400, 405); *12*(12:124–125; 13:176–179, 210–211); *144* (396); *145*(497); *146*(1:659–660, 735)

Reformation *11*(139, 158–159, 165, 167); *35*(108); *44*(69)

Regard *35*(124)

Reindeer *29*(16, 250, 261)

Releife *11*(166); *55*(388)

Rensselaerswyck *75*(434, 437); *75A* (131, 134); *76*(809); *77*(20, 33, 42, 46, 359); *80*(365–367)

Resolution *1*(414); *11*(172–173); *29* (52–53); *199*(74)

Restauration *11*(141); *107*(348–360); *107B*(395–396); *135*(158, 165, 190–191, 200, 232); *141*(237); *144*(177); *145*(258); *146*(1:365); *151*(7:Spring 1956, 39)

Restoration *20*(93); *20A*(64:109); *64* (234)

Retorne *11*(166); *55*(388); *56*(334)

Retriere *29*(114)

Return *1*(208–209, 219, 236–237, 242, 253, 416); *2*(216); *30*(20, 23); *56* (334); *210*(13–14, 24, 41–42, 47, 57); *212*(217)

Reuben *29*(90, 214)

Reuben & Eliza *29*(256)

Revenge *29*(240); *64*(236)

Rialto *64*(294)

Richard *11*(137–138, 143, 167, 171); *56* (332)

Richard & Ann *11*(169)

Richard & Elizabeth *2*(63); *12*(12:124–125, 157, 196); *138*(3:558); *138A*(3:519); *143*(15); *144*(91); *145*(94); *146*(1:126, 128–129); *147*(107)

Richard & James *11*(137–138, 141–143, 145–146, 160–161, 164, 168–169, 171–172, 174); *56*(334)

Richard & John *64*(235)

Richard & Mary *1*(390); *132*(27); *135* (145, 149, 156–157, 164–165, 169, 176, 178, 180–181, 213, 217, 222); *136* (206, 224, 233, 246, 250, 252); *144* (279, 305, 327); *145*(358, 390, 431); *146*(1:487, 531–532, 534–536, 604–608); *147*(107); *151*(6:Spring 1955, 38; 7:Winter 1956, 39); *158*(46); *158A*(61); *175*(180); *176*(465); *199* (74)

Richard & Michael *117*(677)

Richard & Sarah *12*(12:272, 303, 553–554)

Richard & William *117A*(232)

Richard Penn *20*(35–36); *20A*(63:23); *185*(33:475)

Richmond *2*(82, 191, 204); *29*(11–12, 41); *135*(143, 176, 181); *144*(352, 361); *145*(455, 464); *146*(1:684, 695); *151*(8:Summer 1956, 57–58); *175*(183); *233*(188); *233A*(1)

Rigger *29*(92)

Rising States *27*(82); *27A*(Sept 1926:18)

Rising Sun *29*(56, 74, 203, 238)

Rob Roy *29*(217)

Robert *1*(400, 404, 414); *11*(139–140); *20*(174); *20A*(65:247); *29*(20); *63* (6); *63A*(63:182); *64*(230)

Robert & Alice *2*(46, 103, 119, 128, 132, 144, 148, 162, 191, 209); *132*(9, 25, 29); *135*(225); *139*(40); *139A*(5:33); *139B*(9); *141*(236, 238); *143* (17); *144*(134, 143, 157, 164); *145* (159, 189, 203, 233, 245); *146*(1:212–213, 215, 263–264, 267, 270, 286–288, 330, 346–347); *147*(113, 122); *151* (6:Sept 1954, 37; 7:Spring 1956, 39); *159*(21, 24)

Robert & Elizabeth *14*(32); *14A*(65:43)

Robert & Hester *11*(140, 169); *55*(388)

Robert & Oliver *144*(118)

Robert Bonaventure *1*(152); *44*(64); *44A*(339)

Robert Burns *29*(25, 277–278)

Robert Fulton *29*(96)

Robert Lenox *29*(181)

Rockingham *20*(10); *20A*(64:219); *232* (8); *232A*(46)

Roger Stewart *29*(95)

Rolla *29*(87, 131)

Rome 29(26)

Romp 29(143, 149, 215, 222)

Rook Galley 63(178); 63A(67:202)

de Rooseboom 77(54, 127, 251, 359, 414, 416) *See also* Rosetree.

Rosalie 29(255); 243(24–25)

Rosamond 20(33, 88); 20A(63:21; 64:24)

Rosanna 2(28); 135(159, 168, 180, 209, 235); 141(236); 144(162); 145(243); 146(1:343–344); 185(33:475)

Roscius 258(339–340, 343–346)

Rose 1(289); 11(175, 182); 13(6); 35 (184); 44(44); 44A(324); 64(272); 144(390); 145(491, 551); 146(1:729; 3:75–76); 185(33:476)

Rose in Bloom 29(59); 243(24)

Rose of Yarmouth 2(129)

Rose R. Pickle 29(69)

Rosetree 2(10, 72); 83(23); 84(181); 86(40); 86A(154) *See also* de Rooseboom.

Rosetta 145(529); 146(3:22)

Roseway 29(280)

Ross 20(93–94); 20A(64:110)

Rotchell Merchant 11(159)

Rover 25(23)

Rowand 2(120), 161); 139A(5:37; 11–12:84); 139B(13); 144(316); 145 (413); 146(1:568–571, 573); 151(7: Spring 1956, 39)

Roxana 29(222)

Royal Charlotte 20(145–146); 20A(65: 119); 64(248)

Royal Exchange 20(96); 20A(64:112)

Royal Judith 2(11)

Royal Oak 11(168); 29(103, 266)

Royal Union 2(10, 45, 52, 70, 78, 103, 209); 132(24); 139(42); 139A(6: 40); 139B(16); 144(228); 145(312); 146(1:431); 151(7:Winter 1956, 38); 174(9)

Ruby 29(98, 180); 64(254–255, 266, 276, 291)

Rufus King 29(181, 265–266)

Rundell 165(32:368)

Russian Merchant 20(85–86); 20A(64: 22)

Ruthy 29(221)

Rutter 2(121)

S

Sachem 29(200)

Sacred Heart 83(27) *See also* het Gekruijste Hart.

Safety 1(121); 2(28, 41, 84, 90, 164, 172); 217(4:262; 15:143)

St Andrew 2(24, 26, 45, 47–49, 51–53, 65, 68, 80, 95, 113–114, 134–135, 153, 203); 63(174); 63A(67:110); 64 (307); 132(9, 11, 29); 135(133, 180, 232); 136(223); 138(3:614); 138A 3:568); 141(237, 242, 244, 246); 143 15–16, 19); 144(94–95, 108, 125–126, 147, 165, 195, 250–251, 277); 145 (107, 138, 170, 213, 246, 281, 332, 356); 146(1:136, 140–141, 178, 180, 182, 236, 238–239, 303, 305–306, 348–350, 396, 433, 456, 484); 147(108); 151(6:Sept 1954, 37, Spring 1955, 37–38; 8:Summer 1956, 58); 152(63); 154(192); 158(45); 158A(60); 159 (21–23); 163(343)

St Antoine 243(28)

St Bess 20(132); 20A(65:25)

St Clair 29(56)

St George 12(12:228–229); 20(88); 20A (64:24)

St George Merchant 63(6); 63A(63:182)

St Helena 29(64, 203); 238(106)

St Jacob 83(26–27); 84(181)

de St Jan Baptiste 77(428); 83(6, 18), 112(21) *See also* Jan Baptist; John Baptist; St John Baptist.

St John 11(160); 35(204); 56(333); 86(41); 86A(156)

St John Baptist 2(21, 61); 14(14); 14A (64:255); 86(38); 86A(150) *See also* Jan Baptist; John Baptist; St Jan Baptist.

St Louis 242(15:73)

St Mark 2(11, 22); 132(13, 24); 144 (146); 145(210); 146(1:296–297, 299); 147(107, 115)

St Martin 29(10); 78A(338); 78B(376)

St Martyn 78(432)

St Michael 2(191); 145(378); 146(1: 509–512)

St Michael Michael 144(299)

St Peter 2(26); 11(169); 83(27); 84 (181); 86(41); 86A(157)

Sally 2(51, 192, 209); 15(90); 20(76, 78, 121–122, 139); 20A(63:350, 352; 64:321–322; 65:32); 21(50); 24(60: 348; 62:79); 28(205); 29(30, 87, 91, 97–98, 131, 147, 149, 163–165, 223, 245, 257); 36(34–35, 39); 64(245, 247, 249, 256, 260, 264, 266, 269, 272, 275–276, 279, 285, 294, 298, 300, 306–

Index of Ship Names, continued

309, 313–314, 316); *67*(208); *132*(22, 27); *135*(192); *144*(243, 377, 382, 392, 402, 406, 414, 417); *145*(323, 478–479, 484, 493, 503, 506, 514, 517); *146*(1:446, 713, 719, 731, 743, 748, 758, 761); *151*(7:Spring 1956, 38; 8: Summer 1956, 57); *165*(32:246, 353); *185*(33:475)

Sally & Hope *29*(26, 92, 278)

Sally Ann *29*(19, 250)

Salmon *29*(145)

Sam *20*(44); *20A*(63:31); *29*(86, 149); *185*(33:475)

Samaritan *29*(216)

Sampson *1*(212, 247, 250, 262–263); *20* (109, 170); *20A*(64:223; 65:242); *29* (21); *30*(18); *210*(17, 52, 66–67)

Samuel *1*(226); *2*(13, 26, 28, 32, 51, 56, 80, 97, 113–114, 145–146, 199); *11* (171–175); *56*(334); *117*(678, 680); *117A*(227, 233); *132*(11, 30); *135* (200); *138*(3:437, 460, 554); *138A* (3:410, 431, 515); *139*(39–40); *139A* (5:31, 33); *139B*(7, 9); *143*(10, 13, 16, 19); *144*(65, 71–72, 85, 104, 132, 144); *145*(23, 37–38, 75, 131, 184, 204, 541); *146*(1:39, 41–42, 59, 63–64, 106, 110–111, 168, 170–171, 256–257, 258, 261, 289–291; 3:60); *147* (110, 114, 120, 122–123); *151*(6: Spring 1955, 38); *158*(44–45); *158A* (57–58, 60); *175*(180); *199*(74); *210* (31); *211*(72)

Samuel & Betsey *64*(256)

Samuel & Elizabeth *2*(53, 79); *144*(140–141); *145*(198); *146*(1:279–281)

Samuel & Mary *11*(137–138, 142–143, 145–146, 169, 177–181)

Samuel Smith *29*(88)

San Antonio *29*(48, 239)

Sandwich *2*(149); *144*(245); *145*(327); *146*(1:449); *151*(6:June 1954, 40); *174*(9); *175*(176)

Saphire Ketch *11*(163–164, 169); *55* (388); *56*(334)

Sarah *1*(228, 247); *11*(161, 171, 174); *29*(26, 133–134); *57*(30:40); *64*(231, 271, 295); *132*(12, 30); *144*(358); *145*(460, 549); *146*(1:691; 3:73); *159* (22–24); *185*(33:475); *210*(33, 52)

Sarah & Elizabeth *11*(145, 162, 165, 167)

Sarah Ann *29*(266)

Sarah Galley *57*(31:311)

Sarah Sheaffe *252*

Savage *29*(24)

Savary *29*(203)

Schuylkill *29*(48); *193*(462)

Scipio *35*(205)

Scorton Polly *64*(245)

Sea Adventure *2*(219)

Sea Bird *258*(354–367)

Sea Gull *29*(95); *64*(313)

Sea Serpent *29*(245, 270)

Sea Venture *1*(202, 215, 223–225, 231); *208*(xxx); *210*(7, 20, 28–30, 36)

Seaflower *1*(208–209, 223, 236–237, 242, 263); *11*(72, 138, 143); *35*(108); *44* (69); *64*(230, 252, 258, 274, 278, 308, 317); *210*(13–14, 28, 41–42, 46, 67); *212*(217)

Sebella *36*(35) *See also* Sibella.

Semerest. *See* Somerest.

Seneca *29*(15)

Serpent *24*(60:240; 62:78)

Servant *29*(253)

Seven Friends *29*(149)

Seven Sisters *4*(ser 2:141, 155)

Shallopp *185*(33:475)

Shamrock *27*(82); *27A*(June 1926:16–17)

Shannon *28*(205)

Sheild. *See* Shield.

Sherburn *64*(248)

Shield *109*(172); *111*(108); *111A*(379); *117*(673, 678); *117A*(225, 227)

Shipwright *11*(93); *20*(138); *20A*(65:31)

Shirley *132*(26); *135*(179, 186, 199, 204, 216); *141*(237, 240, 242); *144* (247); *145*(330); *146*(1:453)

Sibella *20*(57–58); *20A*(63:234); *64* 267, 269, 272, 275, 283) *See also* Sebella.

Silkworm *29*(13, 219); *243*(27)

Simonds *155*(228)

Sims *20*(106); *20A*(64:220)

de Sint Pieter. *See* St Peter.

Sisters *29*(8, 70, 95, 103)

Six Brothers *67*(207)

Smith *64*(259)

Society *1*(347, 358, 362, 379, 387, 392, 403, 412–413); *2*(73, 168); *11*(136–138, 140–141, 144–146, 162, 165, 168, 172–173, 180–181); *14*(14); *14A*(64: 254); *55*(388); *64*(239); *117*(679); *117A*(228); *199*(74)

Solon *29*(265)

Somerset 64(252)

Sophia 20(106, 108); 20A(64:221–222); 28(206)

Sophia Carolina 145(550); 146(3:73)

Sophronia 29(139)

den Soutberg 76(807)

South America 29(69–70)

South Boston 29(93)

South Carolina Packet 29(7, 18, 33, 124, 244, 274)

Southampton 1(207, 210–211, 217–218, 224, 226–227, 233, 235, 237, 242, 249–250, 252, 258); 2(7, 39, 215); 210(12, 15–16, 21–22, 29, 31–32, 38, 40–42, 47, 54, 57, 62); 211(72); 212(217)

Sparrow 30(19); 35(52, 205); 36(38); 64(290)

Spartan 29(99)

Speedwell 1(82); 2(11, 64, 68, 76, 99, 110, 121, 137, 174, 179); 11(70, 163); 20(37–38); 20A(63:24, 26); 30(13, 204–208); 36(39); 44(77); 54(132); 54A(46–47); 55(388); 57(30:41); 64 (229, 236, 242, 245, 250, 264, 279, 282, 285, 287, 294–295, 297, 300–301, 303, 305, 307, 309, 312, 314, 316); 144 (208); 145(293, 659); 146(1:410; 3: 193); 169(13); 217(2:268)

Spotted Cow 83(5–6, 13–14, 24); 84 (181); 86(36–37, 40); 86A(147–148, 155) See also de Bonte Koe.

Squaril 64(265) See also Squirrel.

Squid 36(37,39); 64(272, 285, 310)

Squirrel 64(292); 141(246); 144(351); 145(454); 146(1:683); 151(6:Spring 1955, 37); 152(64) See also Squaril.

Stamford 64(249, 252, 268, 279)

Star 1(202–203, 205, 213, 218, 231–232, 245, 247, 251); 2(203); 83(25); 84 (181); 86(41); 86A(156)

Starr 11(157–158); 199(74); 208(xxviii, xxxi–xxxii); 210(6, 10, 18, 23, 37, 50, 52, 55, 68); 211(73)

Starr & Garter 20(155); 20A(65:128)

Stativa 243(27)

de Statyn 2(97); 77(80, 132–133, 184, 359, 433); 83(26); 84(181); 86(41); 86A(156)

Stephania 29(14, 273–274)

Stephen 11(141–142, 145–146, 157–158, 160, 164, 172); 20(64); 20A(63:241); 56(333)

der Ster. See Star.

Sterling 29(87); 64(289, 293)

Sterling Castle 36(35); 64(276); 65(15)

Stetin. See de Statyn.

Steven. See Stephen.

Strafford 24(60:241)

Stranger 29(205–206)

Strassburg 262

Strewberry 64(232)

Submission 2(218); 11(136–137); 14 (13, 17); 14A(64:253, 258); 117(674–675); 117A(229–231); 118(7–13); 123 (189)

Success 11(159); 20(37); 20A(63:24); 35(65); 36(37); 39(33–34, 43, 45); 57(30:40); 63(20, 64, 141, 170); 63A (63:272; 64:264; 66:525; 67:106); 64 (236, 252, 254, 257, 259, 261, 270, 274, 286, 299, 314); 144(354); 145(457); 146(1:687)

Success's Increase 20(94); 20A(64:110)

Suckey 20(106); 20A(64:220); 64(305, 308, 313)

Suffolk 29(217)

Sumatra 29(39, 231)

Sunflower 243(27)

Superb 4(ser 1:83); 29(18, 131, 241, 276)

Superior 29(199, 202)

Supply 1(202, 204, 206, 211–212, 222, 257, 364–366, 406); 11(169, 177); 55 (388); 56(334); 210(6, 8–9, 11, 16–17, 26, 62)

Susan 1(224–225, 229, 244–245, 249, 262, 265); 11(160–161); 24(60:25; 61: 134–135, 270); 29(33, 93–95, 97, 227); 109(185); 208(xxxii–xxxiii); 210(29–30, 34, 49–50, 54, 66, 69); 211(72, 74)

Susan & Ellen 1(59, 62, 76); 2(88, 95, 114); 5(2, 6, 39–41, 45, 99, 129, 168, 177–178, 185–187); 35(131, 191); 44 (23, 25, 29); 44A(309–310, 313); 47 (8:258, 260, 263); 50(345); 57(30: 459)

Susan Constant 1(202); 208(xxviii); 210 (7)

Susan Rusher 29(97)

Susanna 1(394, 403); 4(ser 1:86); 11 (160–161, 163–164); 20(8); 20A(62: 246); 36(34); 64(246, 252, 258, 263–264, 276, 279, 294–295, 306–307, 309); 199(74); 243(26)

Suzette 243(23–26)

Swallow 1(246, 358, 374, 394, 404); 11 (182); 36(31, 33–36, 38–39); 64(244, 249, 253–255, 257, 259, 263–264, 267,

Index of Ship Names, continued

273, 275, 278, 280, 283, 289, 291, 295, 301, 307, 310–311); *208*(xxix); *210* (50)

Swan *1*(205, 209, 211, 218, 220, 232, 237–239, 245–246, 248, 250–256, 258, 261–262, 265); *2*(65, 151); *30*(19–20, 22); *35*(52); *208*(xxix–xxxii); *210*(10, 14, 16, 23, 25, 37, 42–43, 50–52, 55–56, 58–60, 62, 65–66, 69)

Swan & Ellen. *See* Susan & Ellen.

Swift *29*(55, 219); *30*(189); *35*(92); *64* (252)

Sybel *29*(226)

Sylvia *64*(301–302)

Syren *29*(143)

T

Talbot *5*(102, 107–108); *35*(60, 65); *39* (33–34, 44–45)

Tekeli *29*(213)

Telegraph *29*(11, 25, 85, 88, 206, 209–210)

Telemachus *29*(53, 215)

Temperance *1*(217, 222, 238); *29*(22, 24); *210*(22, 27, 42)

Ten Brothers *29*(143)

Thames *29*(127–128); *64*(266, 286, 299)

Thane *2*(71); *144*(151); *145*(223); *146* (1:315–316)

Thankful *64*(255, 290)

Themes. *See* Thames.

Theresa *29*(237)

Thetis *29*(89)

Thistle *2*(10, 22, 51, 56, 63, 119); *132* (18, 30); *138*(3:409); *138A*(3:385); *143*(9, 18–19); *144*(62, 121, 127); *145* (20, 163, 172); *146*(1:31, 221–222, 224, 240, 242–243); *147*(120–122); *148–148C*; *154*(191); *175*(180)

Thomas *1*(126); *2*(18, 103, 108); *8*(39); *29*(24, 56); *64*(261, 265, 282, 284, 298) *217*(15:144)

Thomas & Anne *4*(ser 2:149)

Thomas & Benjamin *109*(64)

Thomas & Edward *29*(160)

Thomas & Eliza *29*(87)

Thomas & Elizabeth *14*(43); *14A*(65: 169)

Thomas & John *1*(83); *2*(28, 41, 81, 107, 151); *38*(248); *217*(2:374)

Thomas & Mary *2*(130); *11*(141, 145)

Thomas & Samuel *64*(270, 282)

Thomas & Susan *1*(416)

Thomas & William *35*(91)

Thomas Clackley *146*(3:76–77); *145* (552)

Thomas Gordon *29*(34)

Thomas Tenant *29*(89)

Thorn *29*(38, 238)

Three Brothers *1*(418); *64*(293)

Three Friends *29*(82); *36*(34); *64*(247–248, 265–266, 269–271, 275, 277–278, 281–282, 291, 295, 304, 306–308)

Three Partners *64*(251, 263, 276, 280)

Three Sisters *145*(644, 657, 666); *146* (3:180, 191–192, 204)

Tibitha & Priscilla *14*(37); *14A*(65:49)

Tiger *1*(210, 215, 233–234, 244, 255, 262); *2*(137); *144*(396–397); *145* (497); *146*(1:736); *210*(15, 20, 38, 40, 49, 59, 66); *211*(72)

Tobacco Plant *29*(83, 224)

Tom *145*(591); *146*(3:120–121)

Tontine *29*(60, 198)

Torbay *4*(ser 2:178)

Townshend *2*(68, 77, 80, 191); *141* (238); *144*(109); *145*(140); *146* (1:184–186)

Trader *29*(76, 78)

Transport *1*(101); *2*(14, 55, 63, 74, 79, 84, 91, 127, 150, 155, 172, 179, 213); *4*(ser 1:20); *8*(38); *217*(3:389; 5:343)

Traveler *145*(595); *146*(3:124–125)

Treasurer *1*(206–207, 211, 220, 222, 224, 238, 240, 246, 248, 253, 256, 264); *2* (60, 87); *208*(xxxii); *210*(11–12, 15–16, 25, 27, 29, 43–44, 47, 51, 53, 58, 60, 68)

Trent *1*(397)

Trial *1* (204, 206, 210, 212, 220, 222, 233–234, 252, 255, 259); *2*(136, 176); *11*(141–142, 144–145); *30*(17); *35* (65); *39*(33, 45); *56*(333); *57*(31: 310); *64*(230, 235, 246, 258, 260, 263, 269, 273, 287, 291); *144*(368); *145* (470); *146*(1:703); *208*(xxix–xxx, xxxiii); *210*(9, 11, 14, 16, 25–26, 39, 56, 60, 64); *211*(72)

Trident *29*(63, 191, 257)

Trim *29*(149)

Tristram *64*(271, 277)

Tristram & Jane *9*(142); *219*

Triton *29*(229); *145*(576); *146*(3:98)

de Trouw *2*(153); *77*(117, 190, 208, 274, 282, 359, 409, 413, 419, 426, 428, 431, 435) *See also* Faith.

True American 29(207)

True Britton 64(248)

Truelove 1(85, 131, 209, 211, 213–215, 219, 238, 249); 2(139, 159, 172, 177, 187, 206, 208, 216); 5(8, 10); 7(74); 11(136–138); 35(108, 171); 44(42, 69, 108); 44A(323, 354); 47(8:272); 210(14, 16, 18–20, 24, 42, 54)

Truth & Delight 64(232)

Tryphena 145(581); 146(3:108)

Tuscarora 29(59–60)

Tuyphena. See Tryphena.

Two Brothers 2(11, 13, 26, 40, 62, 64, 67, 74, 77, 195, 206, 216, 219); 4(ser 2: 149); 11(166); 29(74, 207); 36(32) 64 (239, 253–254, 304); 132(11–12); 135 152, 224, 234); 136(221); 141(247–248) 144(179, 184–185, 199, 234, 258, 270–271, 315); 145 (259, 266, 285, 317, 339, 350, 377, 410); 146(1:366, 368, 377, 379–380, 400, 436, 438, 465, 478, 563, 565–566, 568, 675); 147(112, 115–116, 123); 151(6:June 1954, 40; 7:Winter 1956, 38–39, Spring 1956, 39; 8:Summer 1956, 58); 152(66); 155 (228); 169(13); 171(30–31); 173 (13); 174(9); 242(21:965)

Two Friends 20(105); 20A(64:219–220); 28(205); 29(237); 64(254–255, 265, 310, 315); 145(569); 146(3:93); 243(23)

Two Marys 29(10)

Two Sisters 2(121, 161); 36(32); 64 233, 251, 255, 257, 259, 284); 141 (238); 144(117); 145(155); 146 (1: 209–211)

Tyger. See Tiger.

U

Uhland 248(120)

Ulysses 21(41, 62); 232(12–13); 232A (50–51)

Unanimity 20(10); 20A(62:248)

Unicorne 4(ser 1:2); 11(137–139, 143, 160–161, 164, 166, 172, 181–182); 12 (12:161, 191, 193); 56(332); 124 (334, 338); 124A(23); 199(74)

Union 20(35, 72, 160); 20A(63:22, 346; 65:232); 29(138, 145, 147, 218, 274); 64(271, 292); 136(216); 144(409, 415); 145(510, 515, 537–538, 547, 593, 607); 146(1:752, 758; 3:49, 57–58, 70, 123, 138); 151(7:Winter 1956, 39, Spring 1956, 38); 185(33:476);

189(194); 232(4); 232A(42); 238 (35); 242(15:459)

Unity 1(236, 347–348, 366, 384, 404–405); 2(167); 11(140); 29(170–172); 30(21); 35(57); 44(68); 44A(342); 57(33:307–309); 64(230, 247, 249–250, 255, 268, 274, 276, 279, 289, 309); 210(41)

Upton 29(97)

Urania 145(585); 146(3:114–115, 130)

V

Valona 29(161)

Van Stephorst 146(3:47–48); 189(193)

Vanson 64(245, 256)

Venus 20(36, 58); 20A(63:23, 234); 24 (61:138); 29(169, 249, 251–252, 263) 63(45, 175, 213); 63A(63:377; 67: 111, 317); 145(581); 146(3:109)

de Vergulde Bever 77(231) See also Gilded Beaver.

de Vergulde Otter 77(272) See also Gilded Otter.

Vernon 2(154); 144(176); 145(256); 146(1:363)

Verny 135(187); 145(637); 146(3:169)

Vertuous Grace. See Virtuous Grace.

Vestal 29(100, 103)

Victoire 29(235, 238); 243(28)

Victoria 243(27)

Victory 11(166–167); 29(39, 49, 53–55, 146, 150, 215, 217–218, 221, 223, 250, 278)

Vigilant 4(ser 1:83)

Vigorous 64(297)

Vine 2(128, 142, 187); 123(104, 131, 160–161, 230, 505); 124(332); 124A (22)

Vineyard 1(399); 64(233)

Virgin 1(296, 391); 2(161, 175, 186, 206); 64(295)

Virginia 20(6); 20A(62:244–245); 28 (205); 29(58, 88–89, 95, 99, 116, 179, 228, 238, 272); 63(83, 90, 93–94, 99–100, 113, 139, 147, 151, 160, 166, 170–171, 181, 184, 191–192, 194–195, 198–199, 204, 213–214, 219–224); 63A (65:67, 114, 117–118, 123–124, 539; 66:531, 535; 67:96, 102, 106–107, 205, 208, 215–216, 218–219, 222–223, 308, 317–318, 323–328)

Virginia Merchant 12(12:161); 14(18, 30); 14A(64:259, 344)

Virgins Venture 64(235)

Index of Ship Names, continued

Virginus Grace *144*(106–107)
Virtuous Grace *145*(135); *146*(1:175–177); *147*(120–121)
Visitor *29*(103)
Volant *29*(99)
Voltaire *145*(566); *146*(3:89)
Volunteer *64*(246)
de Vos 77(221, 403, 416, 428, 435)
See also Fox.
Vrow Anna *2*(65)

W

W. B. *243*(28)
het Wapen van Noorwegen 76(818)
See also Arms of Norway.
het Wappen van Rensselaerswyck 76 (831)
Warren *29*(54)
Warrington *29*(47–48, 205)
Warwick *1*(202, 206, 219–220, 227, 232, 238–239, 244–245, 249, 253–254, 259, 265); *210*(6, 11, 24–25, 32, 37, 43–44, 49, 50, 54, 59, 63, 69); *211*(74)
Washington *29*(17–18, 245); *243*(28)
Wasp *29*(21)
Water Witch *29*(203)
den Waterhondt 76(822)
Waterloo *29*(48)
Weatherell *64*(296)
Welcome *2*(155, 166); *11*(182); *30* (208); *35*(104); *117*(673, 679); *117A* (225, 228); *119*(467); *120; 121*(152–163); *123*(182, 186, 189, 307, 499); *124*(334, 339); *124A*(23–24)
Wellington *29*(85–86)
Weser *29*(273)
Westpoint *27*(82); *27A*(June 1926:6–7; Dec 1926:29–30); *28*(205–206)
Weymouth *64*(256)
Whale *5*(60, 63, 81, 102, 109); *30*(111); *35*(65, 95); *39*(33–34, 45)
White Angel *30*(189, 352); *35*(60, 93)
White Oak *27*(82); *27A*(Dec 1926:26)
Wicker *29*(267)
Wilhelmine Charlotte *29*(39–41)
William *11*(141, 169); *12*(12:162, 191, 228); *20*(94–95, 105, 116–118, 140, 174); *20A*(64:111, 219, 316–318; 65: 33, 247); *28*(205); *28A*(206); *29*(8–9, 55–56, 155, 252, 257–258); *35* (102); *36*(36); *63*(31, 102, 108, 137, 152, 155); *63A*(63:283; 65:126, 534; 66:521, 536; 67:91); *64*(254, 265, 268, 284, 296); *66*(185); *123*(252); *130*(330–332); *144*(112); *145*(145); *146*(1:194–196); *165*(31:465–466, 470–471; 32:89–90, 93–94); *232*(7); *232A*(45)
William & Anne *4*(ser 2:122); *11*(137–138, 143, 145, 157–158, 161–162, 166, 169, 173)
William & Elizabeth *4*(ser 1:59); *20* (68); *20A*(63:342)
William & Francis *2*(150); *5*(54, 56, 60, 64, 189); *35*(65, 96); *39*(33, 45); *44* 11) *44A*(300)
William & George *4*(ser 2:115); *35* (204); *44*(64); *44A*(339)
William & Henry *29*(152, 247)
William & James *243*(28)
William & Jane *24*(61:348); *29*(256); *35*(102)
William & John *1*(127, 204, 226, 236, 351, 359, 384, 387, 389, 401, 407, 411); *2*(174, 216); *11*(160); *29*(35); *30* (20); *35*(204); *44*(109); *44A*(355); *210*(9, 31, 41)
William & Joseph *11*(168); *29*(57)
William & Mary *2*(201); *11*(171); *12* (12:305, 308, 555; 13:10–12, 46); *24* (62:80); *64*(232, 256, 265); *165*(32: 356–358, 367)
William & Robert *12*(12:192, 196, 228–230, 271)
William & Sarah *2*(17, 21, 64, 77, 146, 190–191); *57*(30:40); *138*(3:300); *138A*(3:283); *141*(235–236); *142*(40); *143*(6); *144*(47–48); *145*(7); *146*(1: 7–9)
William & Susan *1*(350, 358, 373–374, 383, 398–399); *2*(151, 200)
William & Thomas *1*(201, 208, 211, 214, 217–218, 222, 225, 231, 239, 241–242, 247–248, 262, 265); *11*(92); *12*(12: 123); *29*(21, 88); *210*(5, 13, 16, 19, 22–23, 27, 30, 36, 44–46, 52, 66, 69); *211*(72); *212*(217); *215*(132)
William Allen *29*(274)
William Howland *29*(253)
William Johnston. *See* William P. Johnson
William P. Johnson *145*(663); *146*(3: 198)
William Penn *29*(63–64, 89); *123*(309)
Willing Mind *64*(255, 257); *111*(102); *111A*(379); *117*(673); *117A*(229)
Willmott *36*(37); *64*(287); *66*(185)
See also Wilmot.

Wilmington 24(60:347)
Wilmot 29(15, 275) *See also* Willmot.
Wilson 28(206); 29(242)
Windsor 64(307, 316–317); 135(168); 136(207); 144(312); 145(405); 146 (1:555–558); 175(179–180)
Winter Galley 2(56, 73, 113, 140, 190–191); 139(40); 139A(5:32–34); 139B (8–10); 143(17); 144(114); 145(146); 146(1:198, 200, 202)
Winterbourne 64(237)
Winthrop Fleet 5(51)
Wolf 64(251, 313)
Woodcock 20(156); 20A(65:130)
Woodstock 165(30:349, 430)
Woolwich 29(143–144)
Worcester 4(ser 1:78)
Wren 20(125–126); 20A(64:325–326)
Wulfrana 30(112)

Y

Yarmouth 36(32); 64(247, 256)
York 20(123); 20A(64:323); 64(233); 204(57)
York Packet 20(55–56); 20A(63:144, 146)
Yorke Bonaventure 35(56)
Young Haley 29(25)
Young Man's Companion 29(20, 172)
Young William 1(353–354, 360, 364, 366, 383, 392, 402)

Z

Zebeelon 2(211)
Zeno 29(61)
Zephyr 29(56, 216)
Zouch Phenix 35(58)
Zwey Ge Breder 29(17)